Timeless Visions, Healing Voices

Conversations with Men & Women of the Spirit

By Stephan Bodian

Foreword by Joan Borysenko

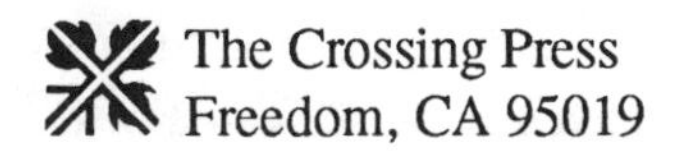
The Crossing Press
Freedom, CA 95019

Photo Credits

Thomas Berry photo by Gretchen McHugh, courtesy of Sierra Club Books

S. N. Goenka photo courtesy of Rick & Gail Crutcher

Susan Griffin photo by Cathleen Rountree

Sam Keen photo by Fred Stimson

Joanna Macy photo by Cathy Busch

Cover design by AnneMarie Arnold
Printed in the U.S.A.

Library of Congress Cataloging-in-Publication Data

Bodian, Stephan.
Timeless visions, healing voices: conversations with men & women of the spirit / Stephan Bodian.
p. cm.
Includes bibliographical references.
ISBN 0-89594-482-0 (cloth) ISBN 0-89594-481-2 (pbk.)
1. Spiritual life. 2. Social problems. I. Title.
BL624.B616 1991
291.4—dc20 91-23933
CIP

Acknowledgments

This book is a collaborative effort. Were it not for the dedication of the sixteen men and women whose interviews appear here, it could not have come into being. In every instance, they gave generously of their time and energy, sitting patiently while I sought to draw from them the accumulated wisdom of a lifetime. Their warmth, candor, and personal presence never failed to surprise and touch me, and in our continuing interactions they have shown the utmost kindness and integrity. To each of them I would like to extend my heartfelt thanks.

In particular, I would like to thank Joanna Macy, the first person I interviewed for *Yoga Journal*, who introduced me to several of the other people who appear here; and Joan Borysenko, who became a contributing editor of the magazine as a result of our meeting and who graciously agreed to write the foreword for this book. Sam Keen and Arny Mindell deserve special thanks for agreeing to be interviewed a second time when the first attempt proved inadequate. Special thanks also to Marion Woodman, who substantially reworked the transcript of our interview to ensure that it accurately reflected her thinking.

Although each of these sixteen men and women has been a teacher to me in some way, two in particular have become teachers in a more formal sense: Arny Mindell, whose process-oriented psychology bridges the (apparent) gap between soul and spirit; and Jean Klein, master of *advaita* (nondualism), whose timeless presence points me back to my own.

Among the friends who have supported me over the years this book took shape, I would like to thank Shepherd Bliss, who first suggested I put together a collection of my interviews; John Welwood, for long walks and soulful talks; Barbara Green, for spiritual sisterhood; and Judith Shiner, for living her truth.

I would also like to express my appreciation to my colleagues at *Yoga Journal*, without whose devotion to the magazine and the values it represents these interviews would have remained mere ideas: Michael Gliksohn, as generous and heartful a publisher (and boss) as one could wish for; Linda Cogozzo, our tireless managing editor; assistant editors Holly Hammond and Anne Cushman; and our art director, Larry Watson.

Finally, I would like to express my love and appreciation to my wife, Laurel Parnell, who has always believed in me.

To Kobun Chino Otogawa,
who first showed me the Way

Contents

Joan Borysenko

Foreword

Rarely have I—and even less rarely has our entire family—enjoyed reading a book as much as this one. As soon as the unbound manuscript arrived, our household of two adults and two young adult sons looked through the table of contents and carved up the manuscript with great anticipation. The range of interviews is superb, from deep ecology to consciousness and psychology. The visions are indeed timeless, as Stephan Bodian points out in the title, but they are also quintessentially timely. The seeds of healing from the separation that has afflicted us on every level—from the environment, to the family, to our own sense of worthiness, to the sacred—are present in these pages.

Each interview is fresh and arresting, capturing the essence of some extraordinary minds and hearts. Having been both interviewer and interviewee at different times in my own career, I've recognized that interviewing is a special, subtle skill—a skill that Stephan Bodian is a master of. Good interviewing requires vision, patience, the ability to question, to listen—the capacity to find the pulse, to feel the lifeblood of the person being interviewed. This Stephan does with apparent ease. Just as importantly, his clear vision has linked these voices into a whole that encapsulates the timeless and the timely into a wondrous compendium that is an education in itself. Were I to recommend a single book that brings together the practical spirituality needed in this critical time, this would be the one.

In testimony to the wide, intergenerational appeal of this book, our sons (young men of eighteen and twenty-two) were delighted—"psyched" as their generation says—to find so many topics of interest to them gathered in the same book. John Robbins' interview, *Diet for a New America*, was scooped up instantly by twenty-two year old Justin, whose reading of it brought him to a new level of commitment in his choice to live as a vegetarian. The Sam Keen article spoke to his interest in the nascent men's movement and his reflections on what it is to be a man. The range of interviews, from S.N. Goenka to Stephen Levine to Bernadette Roberts, on consciousness and spirituality seemed like a treasure trove to this young man who is trying to plumb the heart of the Jewish and Christian heritage, liberally sprinkled with Vedanta that he grew up with.

Eighteen-year-old Andrei was likewise delighted to find interviews with Joanna Macy, John Seed, and Thomas Berry that spoke so strongly to his passionate interest in ecology and a spirituality rooted firmly in the Earth. My husband Myrin laughed and reminisced as he savored every nitty-gritty word of Ram Dass, a teacher that many of us grew up with through the heady, drug culture of the '60s, maturing with him to a more sober but no less joyful, service-oriented spirituality. And I read and reread Bernadette Roberts' extraordinary interview on *The Experience of No-Self.* Although I had read two of her books, this one short interview brought me more deeply into her experience than I had penetrated before.

This is a book full of ideas that will take root in your being. David Steindl-Rast's definitions of prayer and God are like seeds that have already begun to sprout in my own being:

"And that is true prayer: a deep awareness of our limitless belonging—to self, to others, to the universe, to God, to ultimate relativity. In fact, the most basic, most universally satisfying definition of God that I can find is 'the one to whom we belong.' God is the reference point for our deepest sense of belonging."

This is a book that speaks to that belonging. A spiritual book in the deepest sense of the word.

STEPHAN BODIAN

Introduction

In a moment of frustration, as I struggled to piece together an introduction for this book, I wondered whether it needed an introduction after all. Perhaps these conversations—with prominent teachers, authors, healers, philosophers, sages—speak for themselves, I reasoned, and a mere listing of their well-publicized names would be sufficient to introduce what is in fact a diverse collection of interviews conducted over a period of years.

After giving the matter more thought, however, I realized that there is a deeper cohesiveness here, a unifying vision that deserves to be articulated. On one level, it may simply be an expression of my personal vision as editor of *Yoga Journal*, a magazine devoted to health, "conscious living," and the confluence of Eastern and Western ways of thinking, healing, and relating to spiritual issues. These are the men and women whose work piqued my curiosity, and with whom I had the pleasure and privilege of spending a few fascinating hours discussing the issues to which in many cases they had devoted a lifetime of passionate consideration.

As I searched for a title, *Timeless Visions, Healing Voices* seemed as close as I could come to a common quilt to cover such unlikely bedfellows as Sam Keen and S. N. Goenka, for example. Given that the list includes radical environmentalists, cultural reformers, academic philosophers, Jungian analysts, Christian mystics, and Eastern sages, a random observer with an eye on its diversity might understandably dismiss this collection as a potpourri, or worse.

On closer examination, however, a deeper, unifying vision reveals itself behind the diversity of themes. Indeed, it is precisely an allegiance to a sacred unity behind the diversity of the phenomenal world that makes these sixteen men and women kindred spirits. All have been influenced by this vision, which Aldous Huxley termed the "perennial philosophy," the quintessential esoteric current within all religions. Some, because they have experienced its truth so profoundly, have made it the centerpiece of their teaching. These are the sages, the truly "timeless" voices, whose message differs little from the message of their counterparts throughout the ages who have directly intuited its truth. Some are modern Western interpreters of these teachings. The rest have been deeply touched by the perennial philosophy and have allowed it to infuse and inspire their work.

Guided by this perspective, most of the people interviewed here are directly responding, in their writing and teaching, to the planetary crisis of our time. This crisis, they believe, is caused by the resounding failure of the prevailing worldview, which is secular, materialistic, individualistic, and anthropocentric. In contrast, they propose that we adopt a radically different orientation—one that honors the sacred, encourages spiritual expression, emphasizes our interconnectedness, and values all life forms.

According to deep ecologists like John Seed, Thomas Berry, and Joanna Macy, our anthropocentrism and lack of reverence for nature have led us to the brink of disaster. Philosopher Jacob Needleman proposes that the "thing that needs to pass between us"—call it joy, reverence, grace, love— "is no longer passing." Ram Dass urges us to selfless service in the name of the divine. Jungian analyst Marion Woodman concludes that our lack of spiritual sustenance is driving millions to addictions. And psychologist Joan Borysenko criticizes mainstream medicine for its total disregard for the psychological and (particularly) spiritual needs of its patients. Unless we heal psyche and spirit as well as body, she argues, we can never be fully healed.

Each contributor has latched on to a particular piece of the elephant. But unlike the blind men in the parable, these men and women are aware that their perspective is only partial and that the elephant of reality is far vaster than they can comprehend in a single view. What they are proposing, each in a particular sphere of concern, is what science historian Thomas Kuhns has called a paradigm shift, a fundamental transformation of our way of seeing reality. Such a shift took place in the physical sciences many years ago, when the Newtonian paradigm, in which reality was understood as consisting of discrete individual particles interacting according to eternal scientific laws, gave way to a new paradigm in which relativity replaced constancy, energy took precedence over matter, and immutable laws crumbled in the face of unpredictability. Somehow, the rest of us are still struggling to catch up. Unless we do, human life on Earth may be severely endangered.

At a talk I attended recently, Jungian analyst Arnold Mindell discussed the law of entropy, which postulates that a closed system, without outside intervention, will eventually run out of energy like a wind-up toy. But if awareness or consciousness is introduced, the whole picture changes: random interactions become orderly, and the system ceases to be entropic. Our planet is a closed system that is rapidly winding down, Mindell contends. The only way we will be able to reverse this process is if enough people cease to be embroiled in the conflicts that are destroying us and wake up to the reality of our interconnectedness. In the terms of British biochemist Rupert Sheldrake, the formative field generated by such a collective awakening could have an incalculable effect on the prevailing paradigm.

As Joseph Campbell has so eloquently reminded us, the longing to wake up from our consensual trance seems to be as endemic to our species as the desire for food, sex, and sleep. Unfortunately, this "still, small voice" is generally lost amidst the cacophony of competing and apparently more urgent concerns. If we are to follow its gentle promptings toward what Stephen Levine calls the "healing we took birth for," we need constant reminders—inspiration and good counsel—from fellow-travelers on the path. It is in this spirit that I offer these *Timeless Visions, Healing Voices.* May they contribute, if only a little, to our collective awakening—and may they speed you on your own journey of awakening, whatever that may be.

Stephan Bodian
Berkeley, California
April 1991

Joanna Macy

Joanna Macy and I first met at a Passover seder at the home of a mutual friend. Our host, a well-known educator, had gathered together both Jewish and non-Jewish friends for a socially conscious celebration of the joys of freedom and the agonies of bondage. As the ritual played itself out, we were encouraged to contribute from the little store of Jewishness we had gathered over the years: a Hebrew prayer here, an Eastern European melody there, a Hasidic tale, a personal reminiscence of seders past. And through it all ran the conversation—well-informed, heartfelt, and focused on the plight of the Earth: environmental issues, Third World politics, the pre-glasnost threat of nuclear annihilation.

I was already familiar with Macy's work through my involvements in the Buddhist and peace communities, and I latched onto her as soon as we were introduced. At first I was struck by her intensity: she takes long pauses before she speaks and looks at you squarely, with wide, warm, unblinking eyes, as if to say, "Can you possibly realize how important this issue is?" Among her many "important" issues she numbers Central American politics, nuclear disarmament, Third World self-development, Gandhian nonviolence, a radical ecological perspective, and the growth of American Buddhism.

But as we imbibed our obligatory four cups of wine (for such is the Passover custom), Joanna the crusader fell silent and Joanna the playful little girl emerged. No more talk: time for play as zany as the conversation had been intense. By the end of the evening we were all dancing gaily around the room wearing handmade Mexican animal masks, grunting, braying, hugging, and singing, feeling like family and reluctant to part.

Later I thought, "How fitting to first meet this woman, whose principal concern is the interconnectedness of all beings, at a commemoration of our shared struggle with bondage, powerlessness, and despair." Indeed, the work for which she is best known, and which has inspired so many people in this country and Europe, is called despair and empowerment work. Only by first experiencing our despair at the plight of our planet, Macy believes, can we emerge into true personal power.

Macy has been socially and politically active all her adult life. During the early 1950s and again in the early '60s, she worked for the state department (interrupting her career to start a family). In the late '60s she spent five years with her husband and children in the Peace Corps in India, Tunisia, and Nigeria, where she received extensive exposure to the problems of developing nations.

A student of religions since her undergraduate days (she majored in the subject at Wellesley), Macy returned to school in middle age and earned a Ph.D. from Syracuse University for a dissertation entitled "Interdependence: Mutual Causality in Early Buddhist Teachings and General Systems Theory." She seemed destined for a career as a university professor and researcher. But her growing involvement in the antinuclear movement and her encounter with a Sri Lankan self-help organization changed all that, bringing together her two great passions with an urgency that could not be ignored.

"Back and forth I went over the years between these two poles of life, the spiritual and the political," she recalls, "from meditating to public speaking, from preparing testimony on nuclear waste to reading Sanskrit texts. With each passing year the distance between these two poles grew shorter. And when I found my way to the Sarvodaya movement in Sri Lanka, the two paths seemed to converge."

The Shramadana Sarvodaya movement (its name literally means "giving of one's energy for the welfare of all") was begun in 1958 by the young high school science teacher A. T. Ariyaratne as an experimental "holiday work camp" for his students. Soon it had spread to thousands of villages, and today it is a major social and political force throughout this divided island nation. The movement is inspired and informed by the Four Noble Truths of the Buddha—that life is suffering and that there is a cause of suffering, an end to suffering, and a path toward its elimination—and by Gandhi's emphasis on truth, nonviolence, and self-reliance. Sarvodaya calls on villagers to empower and revitalize themselves at a grass-roots level by sharing their resources and improving their own standard of living, rather than relying on the government to identify and solve problems for them.

For Macy, who had already shifted the focus of her political activity from nuclear power to nuclear weapons and had begun to see the potential of the nuclear threat for precipitating deep personal and social transformation, the contact with the Sarvodaya movement was an inspiration. During a year in Sri Lanka on a Ford Foundation grant, she learned that people can be helped to experience their own truth.

"The leaders of the Sarvodaya movement trust the people and their ability to get in touch with their own inner knowing," she says. "They really believe that people already know something is terribly wrong with the world, and that they have the resources and the wisdom within themselves to do something about it. This same attitude distinguishes Interhelp [the organization that has grown up around despair and empowerment work] from other peace groups.

"I also learned from Sarvodaya the importance of listening, to myself and others," she continues. "And I adapted a number of their basic principles—like the four abodes of the Buddha: lovingkindness, equanimity, sympathetic joy, and compassion—to the spiritually based social change work I was involved in here."

This work clearly came to embody for Macy the interdependence she had merely studied in graduate school. Relinquishing her plans for an academic career, she decided to devote herself full-time to giving workshops and presentations on social and spiritual transformation and to serving as a consultant to other like-minded organizations. Today she continues to inspire thousands of creative individuals in their efforts to devise innovative ways of motivating others to trust their own inner knowing. In addition to earlier books on Sarvodaya and despair and empowerment, her published works include *World As Lover, World As Self,* a collection of talks and essays, and *Mutual Causality,* a version of her dissertation.

I met Joanna Macy once more before our interview took place, again at a celebration hosted by a mutual friend. This time we were celebrating not liberation but eros, at a showing of erotic poetry and slides. Lounging against a couch, she seemed perfectly at ease here as well, laughing and joking with several close friends.

Sitting in her kitchen over tea weeks later, we discussed what had happened that evening—how, after the presentation, people had criticized and picked apart their experience out of fear of the erotic.

"And what does the erotic really mean?" she asked rhetorically, leaning forward in her chair. "Just last week I gave a presentation at a conference of theologians and psychologists. Wonderful people, but very much up in their heads. When my turn came, I led them in a totally experiential session that lasted two hours. It brought them out of their heads and into their gut knowing. The next day a Jungian analyst said with excitement, 'The reason your presentation had such a powerful impact is that it introduced eros into our gathering. We all feel so impotent and paralyzed, as if we're sleepwalking our way to destruction. Your work is like the kiss in the fairy tale that awakens the princess from the evil spell.

"'Eros,' he continued, 'is really our capacity to connect—with each other and with the source of life. Until we can experience that interconnectedness, we'll continue to be victimized by our own sense of powerlessness.'"

We paused there, realizing that, with the mention of interconnectedness, we had arrived at the keynote of our conversation together. The interview had already begun.

Joanna Macy

Visions of a Peaceful Planet

Joanna, I see three main areas of involvement in your work: the Sarvodaya Shramadana movement, the antinuclear movement, and deep ecology. And what I see linking all three is your Buddhist practice, particularly the doctrine of pratitya samutpada, *dependent co-arising. Perhaps we could start by talking about what "dependent co-arising" means and what it implies for a way of being in the world and relating to the problems of the world.*

You have a very keen eye. Yes, that doctrine is fundamental to my work. You see, to people engaged in Buddhist practice in the West, the idea of what we wake up *from* seems to be clearer than the idea of what we wake up *to*. We wake up from *greed, hatred,* and *delusion* (ignorance, the prison cell of ego, the sufferings in which attachment embroils us). And when such practitioners consider the alternative—what we wake up to—what most readily comes to mind is *emptiness,* the absence of suffering, one's true nature, which is vacant or featureless.

Yet the Buddhist teachings are very clear, particularly in this central teaching of *pratitya samutpada,* that we wake up to a fundamental realization of the radical interrelatedness, interdependence, and a mutual reciprocal co-arising of all phenomena. It's been very exciting for me to look both at the teachings of the ancient scriptures and at the testimony of modern Buddhist movements to learn more about interdependence and what it it can actually mean for the quality of life. You see, you can begin to experience it right now; you don't have to wait until you're zapped by satori or until you have so many years clocked on the meditation cushion. Every moment can be an invitation to experience this interdependence.

It's very exciting to be alive right now, when new discoveries in contemporary science give us so much grist for the Buddhist mill—whether we're looking at the holographic model of the universe, the bootstrap theory in subatomic physics, or the findings of systems thinkers in the social sciences like psychology, political science, or economics.

Many of the findings of modern science and social science, then, corroborate the teachings of the Buddha on interdependence, discovered through meditative states thousands of years ago.

Yes. In fact, I wrote my doctoral dissertation on *pratitya samutpada* and systems theory. Of course, modern systems thinkers are so conditioned, mentally and emotionally, by a several-thousand-year-old view of reality as composed of discrete, independent substances that we bring those old ways of seeing right into systems theory unless we have a corrective like Buddhist practice. This is where the teachings of Buddha can actually help bring out both the existential and the moral and ethical import of the systems view.

Regarding the moral and ethical implications of the systems view, you have written that the "dynamics of mutual causality . . . would suggest that certain moral values are woven into the fabric of life, intrinsic to its harmony and continuity. These dynamics present, in other words, a reality so structured as to require, for our conscious participation in it, that we live in certain ways." How do you see the connection between dependent co-arising and active involvement in the world?

Many Buddhist scholars in the West—at least 15 years ago, when I was doing my doctoral dissertation—saw dependent co-arising, the Buddha's teaching on causality, as a stumbling block to understanding Buddhist ethics because we have been conditioned to understand moral imperatives as something that must come from an absolute, like commands from on high, either from a deity or from some unchanging essence. But in Buddhism it is actually from the very relativity of dependent co-arising that the Buddhist moral imperative springs, because every action, every word, every thought, every gesture, has reverberations for others and is in some way influenced by everything that is impinging upon it. This reciprocal interaction is so fundamental that we find ourselves co-creating the moment continually.

There's a tremendous responsibility in that.

Yes, responsibility *and* freedom, because in every moment we can choose to have a fresh impact. This is the distinctive feature of the Buddhist teachings of karma: You are conditioned in what you are thinking and doing, but always, in every instant, you can choose.

In my workshops I have used the following story as a unifying theme to link together everything we want to talk about today: the nuclear issue, deep ecology, and Buddhism. It is based on the Shambhala prophesy found in Tibetan Buddhism, about the very difficult, apocalyptic time we are about to go through. Of course, such prophesies exist in other religions as well—the Hindus, the Hopis, certainly Revelation in the New Testament, and so forth.

Among Tibetans this prophesy is given a number of different interpretations. One version sees the prophesy as playing itself out quite literally on the physical plane: The king of Shambhala will come, and all the weapons of destruction will be automatically dismantled. At the other extreme, the journey predicted is entirely internal, to be played out in the psyche only, with little relation to political and social developments.

A third interpretation, the one I find particularly meaningful, was taught to me by me revered friend Choegyal Rinpoche, a Tibetan Lama living in India. According to this version, we are now entering a time of extreme danger in which two great powers, called the Lalös, the barbarians, are locked in mutual hostility. One is in the center of the Eurasian land mass, the other is in the West, and they have, for all their enmity, a great deal in common, including the fact that they have both developed and are manufacturing and deploying weapons of unfathomable death and devastation.

So the future of the planet is in question. And it is at this time that the kingdom of Shambhala begins to emerge. This kingdom is hard to detect because it is not a geopolitical entity; it exists in the hearts and minds of the "Shambhala warriors." For that matter, you can't even tell a Shambhala warrior by looking at her or him—they wear no insignias, badges, or uniforms; they carry no banners; they have no barricades on which to climb or behind which to rest or regroup, no turf to call their own. Ever and always they do their work on the terrain of the Lalös themselves.

Then there comes a time, which we are approaching, when physical and moral courage is required of these Shambhala warriors, for they must go right into the centers and corridors of power, into the very citadels and pockets where these weapons (in the broadest sense of the term) are kept, to dismantle them. Now is the time that the Shambhala warriors must train for this work. And how do they train? They train in the use of two weapons: compassion *(karuna)* and insight *(prajna)* into the interrelatedness of all reality.

This story, and this call or summons to us, unites the branches of the work I've been engaged in. In our "despair and empowerment" workshops this story has had a powerful impact on people from all walks of life, whether or not they have any understanding of or interest in Buddhism.

The training in the first weapon—*mahakaruna*, or compassion—is very important because it frees us from psychic numbing and from the fear of experiencing our own deep responses to the perils of this time. That is, opening ourselves to what is happening to our world—reading a newspaper, switching on the news, letting it in, whether it be world hunger, conflict, war, deforestation, the poisoning of the seas, the nuclear arms race itself triggers in us an anguish for our planet. At the beginning, when I started in this direction five years ago, I called this response "despair." That's not really accurate, because despair suggests to people a lack of hope, and what I'm talking about is an anguish that co-exists with hope. You can be hopeful that we can avert nuclear war or enviornmental catastrophe and still feel tremendous sorrow and anger and guilt and fear about what's happening in our world right now. The term *compassion* seems more appropriate here, because it literally means "to feel with, to suffer with." Everyone is capable of compassion, and yet everyone tends to avoid it because it's uncomfortable. And the avoidance produces psychic numbing—resistance to experiencing our pain for the world and other beings.

In some way, then, the psychic numbing that we're experiencing, particularly at this time, is long standing, something that the Buddha was aware of when he said that people need to cultivate compassion. Precisely that psychic numbing actually prevents us from experiencing our compassion.

You see, the First Noble Truth of Buddhism is dukkha, suffering, and you have to be able to experience suffering if you're going to progress along the path and find the hope and deliverance of the Third Noble Truth, the cessation of suffering. This is true in every religious path, but it's particularly dramatic in Buddhism, because right away you are confronted by that First Noble Truth. Until you can let suffering in, you can't take the next step; you're paralyzed. And it's this paralysis in our time that we break through in doing our compassion work.

The terror that keeps us paralyzed, keeps us subservient and passive, is not our fear of the weapons but our *fear of experiencing* our fear of the weapons. We are afraid of our own deepest responses. We are afraid to look over the edge of the precipice because we don't want to know. Those of us who have done organizing around the arms issue find that it triggers a tremendous amount of resistance. There's resistance in *me* too—I find it hard even to believe that nuclear weapons exist. In a way, it's too ghastly to take seriously.

After all, we've had millennia of civilization—cathedrals, temples, symphonies, Einstein, Mozart, Jesus, the Buddha. And that we are deploying weapons that can blow up the world—or that we are destroying our enviornment at such an alarming pace—is something I find hard to credit. What we need to do to bring us to life, to wake us up, in this situation is to allow ourselves to experience the anguish that's just beneath the surface. We don't have to reach for it, we don't have to invent it, we don't have to cultivate it. All we need to do is to lower our defenses—and breathing helps a great deal, as in certain forms of meditation—and give ourselves permission to take it in. Most of the time we don't allow ourselves to take in the bad news because we think we have to have a solution first. And that freezes us.

So we don't have to have a remedy first before we can face these feelings.

No we *can't.* The trouble is, we put the cart before the horse and don't let ourselves experience the situation unless we have a foolproof solution.

This way of looking at things seems to offer a link between spiritual practice and social involvement. Because spiritual practice is also about grieving, about dropping down into our deepest feelings, the feelings that we're most afraid of experiencing, and allowing them to arise, accepting them, embracing them, making friends with them, and then using them to energize us to move forward in our lives.

This is a time in our society when we urgently need such practices, perhaps more than ever before. We need compassion, for each other and for ourselves, because we're the first generation to have lost the certainty that there will be a future.

That's an inestimable loss.

Yes, and it affects all of us. It's a great unifier, because it's experienced as much in the Pentagon as in the peace movement. It's as much of a loss for Dick Cheney as for Daneil Ellsberg or for you or me.

Would you say that Dick Cheney, for example, with all his inner defenses, is experiencing the despair that each one of us is experiencing but is unable to contact that feeling?

That's my assumption. I've worked with about 12,000 people, and I haven't met anyone who, at some point, at some level, doesn't feel some pain for the world, regardless of what policies he or she may advocate for dealing with the world situation. No one can deny that our future is in danger, even if they think the chances of that danger are relatively small. You see, every generation throughout recorded history has lived with the assumption that other generations would follow and that the work of their hands, their heads, and their hearts, would be carried on by their children and their children's children. That assumption gave meaning and a sense of continuity to their lives. Failures, sufferings, even personal deaths, were ever encompassed by that vaster assurance of continuity.

It's precisely that assurance that we've suddenly lost. Robert Lifton calls that the "broken connection" and talks about it as a sense of radical biological severance that affects every relationship at some subliminal level. But among kids now it isn't all that subliminal—they *talk* about their sense of futurelessness; it affects their ability to make long-term commitments and long-term relationships.

The Greeks had two words for life—one was bios, *and the other was* zoe. Bios *was individual life, and* zoe *was that continuity, that ongoing eternal stream stretching from beginningless past to endless future. One could rely on that continuum underlying everything.*

That's a very helpful distinction. What we fear now is much more that personal death; it's the death of *zoe.* And we have hardly any words or images for the anguish we feel over this.

How do you work with people around their despair, to cut through their psychic numbing?

Usually the work is more effective in groups, because of the energy that's released. It's important for people to see that what they're experiencing is not private but is very widespread. A simple way to begin is to give people the opportunity to acknowledge and express the feelings they carry around with them about what is happening to their world. In order to do that, those feelings have to be validated as a normal, natural, human response—indeed, as a measure of one's humanity. The assumption of any people growing up in this culture, which is so focused on optimism, is that "I must be crazy to feel this distress."

For example, I often begin with a breathing exercise, an adaptation of the *bodhicitta* meditation, which is an ancient practice designed to enhance the capacity to experience compassion. I just talk people through it—perhaps with some music to relax their defenses against their awareness of suffering. Focusing on the breath, we experience how the stream of air passing through their bodies connects us with the living, breathing web of life. Letting images of the world's pain arise in our minds, we breathe them through on that stream and visualize them passing through the heart. For the moment we are asked to do nothing more. The permission simply to register this pain—without having to produce a foolproof solution to the environmental devastation, without having to win an argument—opens profound levels of knowing and caring. At the close of the practice, people share some of the images that have come up for them, often with great emotion.

Frequently I'll move away from words and work with music, imaging, colors, and drawing to elicit the feelings. Because talk can be a great way to avoid our experience. As people allow themselves to experience, a catharsis comes, in which a great deal of energy is released—energy that was devoted to the repression of those emotions. Hilarity may emerge as well, including dancing and laughing and eruptions of joyousness—probably because of the sense of bonding with others and the release of feelings long withheld.

That's important to hear. I think people often wonder, "If I allow those feelings to come up, won't they overwhelm me? Won't they be more that I can handle?"

Precisely. That's where working with the breath and where dependent co-arising and systems theory are central. They allow us to say with confidence, "If I have these feelings, I'm not going to shatter into a thousand pieces." It is only when we hold our pain for the world at arm's length that it solidifies, and we're stuck with it.

Through shared pain also comes a sense of connectedness, and—through this connectedness—laughter, affection, and celebration. When we allow ourselves to experience our compassion, which is grief with the grief of others, we get to experience the other side, too, which is joy in the joy of others and power in the power of others. So we always do some work redefining power, looking at how what we've just experienced flies in the face of the patriarchal notions of power—power over, power as domination, power from the top down.

That's why you call your work despair and personal power.

Right.

The other side of getting in touch with your despair is empowerment.

The very process of moving through to the despair gets us in touch with the interconnectednesss that is the source of true power.

I often use the metaphor of the neural net. I ask, "What is the power of a nerve cell?" Is it, "I win, you lose"? Is its power enhanced by the weakening of the nerve cell next door? Can it be equated with invulnerability, with erecting defenses?

You see, I know, given what I have to do and what we all have to do to heal the world, that I don't have enough love, or courage, or intelligence, or compassion, or endurance, to do it on my own. But I don't need to. Because if we're all interpenetrating and interexisting, then I can draw on your intelligence and your courage and your endurance. I learn to view your strengths as so much money in the bank, which gives me a tremendous sense of buoyancy in doing the work.

So the pain of the world and the power to heal it come from the same source, turn on the same pivot or hinge, which is our deep ecology—our interconnectedness.

What about the second weapon, prajna, *or wisdom?*

Choegyal Rinpoche, the Tibetan teacher who told me the Shambhala prophesy, also stressed that each of the two weapons is necessary; one without the other is insufficient. Compassion by itself risks becoming sentimentality and can be hard to bear, can even breed divisiveness. That's why we need the other—insight into the interexistence of all phenomena. But that insight by itself is also inadequate; it becomes too abstract and cold and needs the "passion" of compassion. And the compassion, the suffering, makes the second weapon experientially real to people. People can really believe in their pain.

As we allow ourselves, in the workshops, to experience our anguish for the world, our grief over the death of *zoe*, or our suffering now with our fellow beings, there comes a time when I point out, "Please note the extent to which this pain that you're sharing, these concerns, expand beyond your concerns for your own separate ego, your individual needs and wants. That says something very important about who and what you are." If they go into that pain, participants find that it's rooted in caring, and that caring comes from our interconnectedness. And so we open to the fact that we suffer with our world because we belong to it, like cells in a larger body.

And that is the birth of prajna.

Right. And you can *believe* it. It's no longer some noble, Olympian notion. It becomes a living reality. Deep ecology seems to be a wonderful way to talk about our interexistence, our dependent co-arising. The main metaphors we use are body metaphors—we are awakening to our co-participation in the larger body.

You've talked about deep ecology several times in our discussion. Can you explain how it differs from regular environmentalism?

Deep ecology encompasses all aspects of life and does not measure the dangers or the actions we must take in terms of what they mean for our species alone. A lot of environmental actions and concerns arise around, and are justified in terms of, how they affect our well-being as *homo sapiens.* "We must stop polluting our rivers because we'll get cancer," or "We must stop cutting down the tropical rainforest because it will change the climate for *us.*" The perspective of deep ecology posits a very basic shift in identification—identifying beyond the individual and his or her separate needs to the planet itself, to all life. It recognizes—on a level that makes me suspect that most deep ecologists have had a mystical experience at some point in their journey—that all life forms interweave to create a biosphere that is a living organism, a single mind. The British scientist Lovelock has called this organism Gaia, one of the names of the Earth goddess in classical mythology. According to Lovelock the regulation of salt in the seas, the regulation of oxygen in the air, and countless other phenomena can only be explained if we consider Earth a living being. And people are ready to experience this. They see it as an escape from the constrictions of separate selfhood, as a kind of coming home.

You see, the watershed came when we were able to see our planet from the outside. Those photographs from the moon allowed us to see ourselves as this exquisite silver-blue jewel dangling in space, so fragile, so lovely, so seemingly alive. We began then to fall in love with our planet.

Sometimes in our workshops I pass around a large ball of our Earth that people can hold, and I invite them to talk to it, to address it as "You," either silently or out loud. This gives them the opportunity to tell their planet how much they care about her, how much they need her, and how they feel about what's happening to her now. People find this very natural, and very moving as well.

I have one last question, Joanna. In light of the issues you've raised, how do you see religious life evolving in the future?

Judging from my experience in workshops, I think more forms will arise outside of the churches, places where people can create rituals, can teach each other, can do religious practices. And I am haunted by the suspicion that there will be new centers of nonsectarian religious life that will have some relation to the need—even if we dismantle every weapon tomorrow—to protect our radioactive reactors and sites for the next several hundred thousand years.

Why will they need to be protected?

To save us from genetic mutations and cancer epidemics of fearful proportions. Those radioactive piles and the wastes and tailings will have to be guarded from looting, misuse,and negligence for the next quarter of a million years. I believe that the task will require such rigor and fidelity that it could only be a religious vocation. I foresee a form of lay monastic life arising around those sites. And I predict that people will make pilgrimages there, to remember that we almost ended the human story, and that we can still destroy our world. The "re-membering" will be a spiritual, a religious act.

You are envisioning a complete transformation of the materials of potential destruction into a source of religious inspiration. That's a remarkably hopeful vision.

Yes. There's no reason why we can't wake up and allow that to happen. Certainly no technical reason. But I don't think it will be cheap. Given our blindness and our resistance, we won't get there without a lot of suffering. But I believe we'll make it.

John Seed

John Seed is probably the world's most outspoken rainforest advocate. The indefatigable Australian has buried himself in the path of bulldozers, camped out in tall trees, and otherwise placed his body on the line to protect these threatened ecosystems, which harbor over half the world's plant and animal species and provide us with irreplaceable oxygen, foods, medicines, and other raw materials.

Since the mid 1980s, Seed has traveled to the Solomon Islands, Malaysia, India, New Guinea, and throughout Australia in support of rainforests under siege. In the summers he has led rainforest roadshows in the U.S., showing videos, playing music, and staging "community therapy" events called Councils of All Beings, in which participants take the part of plant and animal species and speak to the humans who endanger them.

Stanford biology professor Paul Ehrlich has called Seed "a tremendous example of what a person without strong professional training in ecology can do by becoming informed, and then becoming an activist." *The Christian Science Monitor* has dubbed him "the town crier of the global village."

Seed is former editor of the *World Rain Forest Report*, a newsletter providing up-to-the-minute information on the atrocities being committed against rainforests worldwide, and is the founder of the Rainforest Information Center, an organization that has inspired the creation of similar groups in other countries, including the Rainforest Action Network in the U.S.

Yet Seed never anticipated becoming an environmental activist. Introduced to Tibetan Buddhist and vipassana meditation while traveling in India in the early '70s, he returned to Australia to help start Bodhi Farm, now a thriving Buddhist community in a forested area of New South Wales. By 1979, his life revolved around family, community, organic farming, and spiritual practice, which consisted of morning and evening meditation and two 10-day retreats a year.

Then one day Seed's life underwent a profound and irrevocable transformation. "There was a dispute over logging at the end of Terania Creek Road, only four or five miles from my home," Seed recalls. "To show the level of my disinterest in such matters, I had never gone to the end of that road and had no idea there was a rainforest there.

"I can't remember what motivated me to go. I've tried to, because it was such an important turning point in my life. From that moment on, everything changed. Maybe it was the combination of experiencing the rainforest itself, which is totally different from the regrowth forest at Bodhi Farm, and the heightened circumstances of civil disobedience, danger, and arrest. No one else was affected the way I was."

Within a short time, Seed's meditation practice fell away, and he became consumed with a passionate love of the rainforest and, through it, of the rest of the planet. "The rainforest led me to the mangroves and the marshes and all the wild places in nature." The civil disobedience at Terania Creek, which Seed helped lead, lasted for many months, resulting in hundreds of arrests, and grew to include surrounding forests as well. The action gained such widespread media attention that eventually over 70 percent of the residents of New South Wales indicated they wanted an end to rainforest logging. Ultimately, the "best half" of the rainforests in the state were preserved in a series of national parks.

But for Seed, Terania Creek was only the beginning. At the invitation of other environmental groups, he spearheaded a series of actions throughout Australia that resulted in legal protection for most of the country's precious rainforest preserves. Perhaps the most dramatic of these was a massive campaign to stop a huge dam that would have flooded a prime temperate rainforest in one of Australia's wildest areas. The complex, months-long blockade drew over three thousand people, the largest environmental action in the country's history. After 1,500 arrests, again with extensive media coverage, Labor Party leader Bob Hawke promised that, if given the majority in the forthcoming election, his party would stop the dam. Thousands of environmentalists campaigned door to door, the Labor Party won, and Hawke's first words after his victory were: "The dam will not be built."

Despite his impassioned advocacy of nature, however, Seed spent years trying to reconcile his environmental involvement with his spiritual beliefs. "There was the feeling in Buddhism that one should stay cool and not get heated up about things," he explains. "Many things happen in the world, but you just watch them come and go. I found myself doing certain things because I needed to, but a part of me felt I was going astray." Not until he discovered the philosophy known as deep ecology—in the writings of Zen teacher Robert Aitken, environmental philosopher Arne Naess, and poet Robinson Jeffers—was Seed able to achieve the integration he sought.

If the urgency of his message has taken its toll on Seed, one would have a hard time judging from his appearance. Dressed in shorts and a t-shirt during our interview despite the cool spring weather, he seems relaxed, centered, and a bit bemused. Like Buddhist monks I have know, he has apparently managed to leaven his intensity with the knowledge that, despite the grave problems we face, our world has its own inherent perfection. We begin our interview with "deep ecology," the philosophy that guides Seed's work.

John Seed

Rainforest Man

What exactly is deep ecology?

Deep ecology is a new philosophy of nature that provides the most radical critique of the Western ideology of progress and development that I know of. It takes a biocentric approach, which is the opposite of the anthropocentic view that most of us hold. Just as Galileo and Copernicus showed that the belief that the Earth is the center of the universe is false, so deep ecology shows us that the idea that humans are the center of the universe, the source of all value, the crown of creation, is false. The science of ecology teaches us—as do the traditions of native and natural peoples and to some extent Taoism, certain kinds of Buddhism, and other Eastern strains of thought—that the world is not a pyramid with one species (ours) on top, but rather a web of which we are one strand interconnected with all the other strands.

Deep ecology welcomes the support of environmental movements that are based on a "shallow" ecological perspective. For instance, a resource-based environmentalist, one who believes that the world is composed of resources for human beings and that the only value anything has lies in its usefulness to us, may work to make sure that these resources are used in a wise and sustainable fashion. Such a person may be aghast at the destruction of tropical forests because, properly managed, these forests could be a resource not just for us and our children, but for many future generations. As a result, this person may struggle alongside us to protect those forests.

But there's a world of difference between this position and the position of deep ecology, which holds that these forests, far from being a resource, are the matrix out of which we and all other life forms grew; that for a hundred million years I was molded by these very forests, emerging just a few million years ago onto the plains; and that my intelligence, which I prize so highly, is just a tiny subset of the intelligence of this rainforest, which gave birth to it, and an even tinier subset of the intelligence of Gaia herself, the integrated, fuctioning living being which is our planet.

So deep ecology is a spiritual view of nature, one that sees an incredible richness and miraculousness everywhere. It takes the creation myth of science, which originated with Darwin, and infuses it with the kind of feeling other cultures have for their creation myth.

Deep ecology—and in particular the deep ecology rituals that a number of us have developed—is an attempt to move human beings from center stage to what Aldo Leopold calls being a "plain member of the biotic community." Nothing special.

This view is becoming more and more acceptable intellectually, but it doesn't easily lead to the kinds of life-style changes that are going to be needed. Our anthropocentrism is so deeply ingrained. We behave as though the world were a moral testing ground for human beings; as though the things that are happening to the world aren't really happening; as though there were some other reality that we could drop back into, and that, if we were to destroy this world, it would not be ultimately important. If we really did believe it was important, we'd have to change our lives in some radical ways. But we don't.

Not only Christianity, but all the major world religions support the view you're describing. For example, Buddhism teaches that everything is ultimately empty of an abiding self-nature. Human beings, the whole planet, can come and go, but it doesn't matter at an ultimate level.

There is a level at which I accept that as well. Once there were just rocks and dust with an inherent ability and propensity to weave themselves into stuff like this [pointing to his body], and that's not going to be touched by anything we do. There's an ultimate sense in which it *is* all empty and unimportant.

I imagine that must give a certain levity to what you do.

It does. It means that I can look that hole in the ozone layer square in the eye without the kind of counterproductive hysteria often associated with the peace and environmental movements. It's good to be able to face the truth without panic. Ultimately every atom of every molecule that composes me and all the things I love has always been here. It was here in the Big Bang, thirteen and a half billion years ago, and it was here when the Earth was created four billion years ago; it's indestructible. There's a miraculous, indestructible layer underlying everything.

What you were saying about religions supporting this view reminds me of a story I once heard about Gary Snyder. Snyder worked in Jerry Brown's office when Brown was governor of California in the 1970s. At a certain point Brown asked Snyder, "Gary, why is it that you always go against the flow?" Snyder replied, "What you call the flow is just a 16-thousand-year eddy. I'm going with the real flow." All those religions are going against the real flow by attempting to push human beings above the nature that has been our matrix for so long.

When looked at on a 24-hour "cosmic clock" of the Earth's history, this attempt to separate ourselves out, to make ourselves different, seems very presumptuous. On this clock, life emerges at 5 p.m., mammals at 11:30, and the human species at a few seconds to midnight. All the ideas we have about ourselves, all our philosophies and religions, emerge a couple of hundredths of a second before midnight and ignore the rest of the 24-hour period, except this modern creation myth, this modern religion of science.

I agree with Brian Swimme, Matthew Fox, and Thomas Berry about the importance of telling this myth, this cosmic story, because it's a truer story that encompasses all the others, and it's perhaps the only story that all of us humans can agree upon.

If we don't agree upon it in the next few decades and fit our millionth-of-a-second recent stories into it, we're going to be the last human generation that has a chance to do anything about the environmental crises that face us—the destruction of the rainforests, the ozone layer, the greenhouse effect, pollution, toxic wastes. I've studied all the statistics quite intensively for the last 10 years, and it's quite clear that, unless we fundamentally change within our lifetimes. no future generations of human beings will be able to save us. None of the conservation efforts that are taking place now, even multiplied by a factor of 10 or even 100, will be enough to stop the deterioration of the biological fabric out of which we, and all life, have been created. If we become very, very wise and increase our conservation efforts tremendously, we might eke out another 10 or 100 generations of human beings. But after four billion years, that's just a flash. There are tree species whose individual members live that long.

We need a deep ecology perspective that allows us to experience our *actual self* stretching back over these vast periods of time. We need to experience the significance of the fact that my blood has such a similar composition to the composition of sea water hundreds of millions of years ago that I could be seen as a piece of the sea that surrounded itself by a membrane in order to come out onto the land. That sea still flows through my veins. We need to see this, not poetically or scientifically, but as our identity, so that when people say "I," they are referring to this much vaster reality.

I'm not a nature mystic who spends as much time as he can out in nature. I spend far more time on the word processor defending nature than I do worshipping her. But if I'm confused or not quite sure what to do, I go out into a forest for a few days, maybe cover myself with leaves, and consciously surrender and ask for guidance and empowerment from the great wisdom that gave rise to me and that exists in that forest. Then my sense of who I am changes.

As my sense of my self has changed, my self-interest (which is very strongly developed and has always motivated me) and my way of expressing that self-interest has also changed. To be defending the rainforest has become a matter of self-interest, not a matter of sacrifice or pride. People sometimes say to me, "You're certainly a very noble spirit, doing such things."

Whereas it's almost as natural as defending your family.

Exactly.

Given the fact that the biosphere is deteriorating so rapidly that radical action is necessary, what do we need to do to prevent that from happening? Obviously it isn't enough just to recycle our glass and aluminum and cut down on the meat we eat.

I'm not sure how much it's a matter of "doing," at this point. It seems to me that nothing short of a total revolution in human consciousness is going to be of any use. There has to be a really profound spiritual change, beyond anything that one can point to in written history—beyond Christ, beyond Buddha.

I've read somewhere that hundreds of thousands of people became enlightened during the Buddha's lifetime. Unless all human beings become enlightened to their true nature—which is none other than the nature of this planet, Earth—within the next few decades, deterioration of the life-support systems (in particular, the tropical forests, which are the lungs and the circulatory system of the Earth, and the ozone layer, which protects us from harmful radiation) will continue at such a rate that none of our present efforts at conservation will save us. The only thing that will save us, it seems, is an almost instantaneous awakening within human beings as to where our true self-interest lies—something that will be so enlightening that all our present religious and cultural conflicts will just fade into a kind of mist.

I'm not suggesting that I believe this will take place. But it's my considered view that nothing less is worth struggling for at the moment, because nothing less will do the trick.

It reminds me of a story about Mulla Nasruddin, the divine Sufi fool. The Mulla is down on his hands and knees beneath a lamppost, searching for his keys, when a friend comes by and offers to help him. After some time the friend remarks, "Well, neither of us can find the keys. Are you sure you dropped them here?" "Actually," replies Nasruddin, "I dropped them over there, in the dark, but it's much easier to look for them here." Often I think we get involved in a particular issue because it's just too dark where the actual problem lies.

In particular, I've come to realize that information alone is not sufficient. Every taxi driver I speak to has the information, but it doesn't make anywhere near enough difference. We need to experience the plight of the environment as a life-threatening situation. Unless we do, and leap back as one from the brink of extinction (and not just our own extinction, but the extinction of so many beings with whom we've co-evolved over millions and millions of years), then a vast simplification is inevitable.

Whether this simplification, this peeling back of the complexity of life on Earth, will involve the destruction of the mammals only, or the destruction of all vertebrates—how far back it will go is anybody's guess. Perhaps we'll destroy all the oxygen, and life will become anaerobic again, as it was billions of years ago. Or perhaps only sterile rock will remain. I don't know. But I haven't the slightest doubt that the biological richness and density necessary to support large mammals such as ourselves will be utterly destroyed within a few decades unless this huge change occurs. Anybody who seriously studies the matter and doesn't bring forth some kind of supernatural intervention ("Someone's going to come from space and rescue us") inevitably concludes that unless we pull ourselves back from the brink, we've had it.

We have this tremendous pedigree: For four thousand million years we've survived, along with everything else that survives now. It's as though we've been tossing a coin for four billion years, and it's come up heads every time. That's quite miraculous, because as soon as you toss tails, you're out of the picture—only a fossil record remains. The species that exist now are the ones that were able to successfully adapt. They have a good track record. And this gives us some reason to hope that the 16-thousand-year written history of wars, slavery, and torture is not the end of the story—that, if we can come to realize what is required of us today, we might be able to come up with the goods.

Of course, things are changing much more rapidly now than ever before.

That's right. And the change that's required is a spiritual change, rather than a change in body chemistry or genetic makeup.

Evolutionary leaps usually take quite a long time, because they require, at least according to the theory, that certain mutations occur that allow the species to adapt. Now we're being asked to change within several decades. But, as you say, this is a spiritual, not a physiological, change.

And there is evidence that spiritual change is instantaneous, at least on the individual level. Whether such a thing could be extrapolated to a whole species is another matter. I wouldn't say that such a mass spiritual transformation is likely, but it *is* imaginable. Over the last 10 years, human beings have for the first time been willing to consider the possibility that extinction may be our fate—and soon—in our lifetime or our children's lifetime.

We quickly push this thought away again, of course. But we need to look over the abyss into the possibility of extinction and not shy away with dreams that spaceships are coming to get us or that the new age is upon us and everything is going to be all right. The evidence shows just the opposite.

What would this massive evolutionary leap look like, if it were to happen?

For a start, it would mean that every time we went out into nature, we wouldn't be extracting things. In spite of Moses coming down from the mountain and breaking the tablets, and in spite of Christianity, we still worship Mammon, still worship material goods. It's one of the most pious religions the Earth has ever known. We believe that what comes out of the ground has no value until we, through our immense cleverness and ingenuity, give it value. The Earth is incredibly generous; we can get just about anything we want from it. We can take a bit of dirt and extrude it into steel, or turn oil into plastic and send it to the moon. We need to replace this secular religion with a worship of something other than ourselves and our handiwork—the worship of what gave rise to us. We need to go out into nature not to extract or improve something, but in a spirit of worship. We need to be receptive to the miraculousness and the wisdom and beauty of nature, trying to leave it richer rather than poorer as a result of our traveling through it.

The heroic human urge to make things better could be used to invite the wildness back. Because far more wild nature is needed for the long-term continuation of the Earth. What Paul Ehrlich calls the "free services" provided by the Earth—the hydrological cycle, the circulation of fresh water, the oxygen cycle in the atmosphere, the soil cycle, the creation and maintenance of soils that produce our food—all depend upon the wild. We haven't created them, and we couldn't reproduce them if they were destroyed.

This leap also involves seeing ourselves as a much longer and larger thing than we had thought. Wildness goes back four thousand million years on this Earth, and stretches forward potentially for four thousand million years more, which is how long some say it will be before the sun goes into nova. We're only halfway through our journey; vast adventures await us, and vast populations of humans, but not all at the same time. We could have 20 billion humans all at once and then leave a piece of charred rock to spin through space for four thousand million years. Or we could have 200 billion humans stretched over millions of years.

So the first thing we need to do is to invite the wildness back, not by planting things, but by respecting the wildness that remains and by restoring the conditions whereby nature can renew herself and thereby renew us as well. For example, we could take wild areas that have fallen below the size judged necessary for their continued survival and viability and start to fence them off to keep out cattle, fires, and other external forces. We could allow them to reestablish themselves and express their nature, rather than imposing our will on them.

There's a lot of work to do. This leap we're talking about would also require us to start using so much less. The sense of well-being and self-esteem we presently get from surrounding ourselves with material things we would have to find elsewhere—for example, in our relationships with one another, in our relationship with nature, or in our philosophy or spiritual pursuits.

The missing variable in our discussion so far, it seems to me, is population. We are now five billion strong and could conceivably grow to 11 billion by the year 2100. How can we stop population from growing so fast? No matter what we do, if the population continues to grow at the present rate, all our efforts will be wasted. In Kenya and Tanzania, for example, the government tries to support and protect the wild animals in its national parks, but population density on all sides is so great that animals are being poached at an alarming rate—antelopes for food, elephants for ivory, and so forth. How do we prevent this tremendous press of population?

First of all, I see it not as a population problem alone, but as a problem of the relation between the number of people and how much each of them consumes. Otherwise, it's politically impossible to do anything about it. The zero-population-growth and other similar movements of 10 or 20 years ago foundered over the fact that the people in the developed world, who only had an average of 2.2 children, were trying to get people in the underdeveloped world, who had an average of six or seven children, to change their ways, when those 2.2 children consumed 10 times as much of the Earth's resources as the other six or seven. At the moment, my child or your child might consume as much as 50 Indian children. It's more important for us and our children to consume less than for Indians to breed less. We have to reduce the population and *increase* the per capita consumption in the poorest places in the world, while reducing the population and *decreasing* the per capita consumption in countries like America and Australia.

Here again, a spiritual change needs to take place. My desire to procreate myself as an individual must be effortlessly subsumed in my species survival instinct, in my wish for the survival of that larger organism of which I'm a part.

Earlier you used the phrase "to invite" change, rather than to cause it.

Yes. The rituals that I and others lead are an invitation. They're a kind of spiritual activity, a prayer. Sometimes I think that everybody knows what I'm talking about, but they've decided that it's too hard to do anything about it. So they're going to commit suicide, but they don't want to tell the children, and they're trying to invent pills that will make it a little less painful.

I don't agree. I want to keep going. I put all my energy into my prayer that this beautiful, blue-green planet will keep spinning through space. I also pray, but with less energy, that human beings will be included, because I don't mind if the Earth goes on without us. I'd rather it didn't. I like human consciousness. But it's really minor compared to the biological fabric that gave rise to humans. In a few million years that fabric has thrown up humans, and it can do the same again. If it remains intact, there's hope for the future. But without it human life means nothing.

Thomas Berry

Even as a child, Thomas Berry could foresee the global gridlock toward which the industrialized world was hurtling—and he knew he would be destined to help think it through. Raised Catholic in predominantly Protestant North Carolina, Berry had an early aversion to automobiles, which were just being introduced to his part of the world, and he spent as much time as possible in the woods. The Earth was being oppressed, he realized, and only by "orienting to the total Earth process" would he one day be empowered to do anything about it.

After a brief stint at a Catholic college, Berry spent 10 years in a monastery in Massachusetts, then returned to school to complete a Ph.D. in history because he wanted to understand how "human beings discovered their sense of reality and value." After several years as a college teacher in Peking and several more as a NATO chaplain in West Germany, he returned to the U.S. in the early '50s, teaching history and Asian studies at various Catholic universities until his retirement in 1979. Among his special interests have been Chinese, Indian, and Native American cultures and the philosophy of French theologian Teilhard de Chardin, whose ideas deeply influenced his own. For many years Berry served as president of the American Teilhard

Association; today he heads the Riverdale Center for Religious Research, just up the Hudson from New York City.

As a geologian (a term he prefers to "theologian"), Berry's chief concern has been to shift the emphasis of religion from God-the-Father-in-the-sky to the universe as an infinitely creative manifestation of divine presence. Indeed, according to Berry, the biblical story we keep telling ourselves about the cosmos—that we are specially chosen by God to have dominion over nature—has led us to exploit the Earth rather than cherish and protect it. Instead, he counsels, we must adopt a "New Story" that celebrates the sacredness and interdependence of the entire creation. Governed by a primordial "dream" whence all things come into being, the universe, he suggests, is a constantly evolving, self-organizing process that we must learn to participate in, rather than control.

The following interview took place in a small office at the Institute for Culture and Creation Spirituality in Oakland, California, the college founded by Berry protégé Matthew Fox and dedicated to the exploration of the "New Story" in all its expressions. Although the conversation focuses chiefly on the ways in which Berry was influenced by Teilhard, it manages to elicit the core teaching of one of the seminal Christian thinkers of our day.

Thomas Berry

Dream of the Earth

The French theologian Teilhard de Chardin had a powerful influence on your thinking. Could you talk a little about that.

He influenced my thinking in three basic ways. He was the first person to tell the story of the universe as a psychospiritual as well as a physical reality from the beginning. He identified the human story with the universal story. And he shifted the religious emphasis from redemption to creation. The limitation of Teilhard was that he had no real ecological sensitivity and he had excessively high expectations of technology and science.

As far as the story of the universe is concerned, there had been idealistic interpretations before his that challenged the notion that the universe is merely a mechanism, but none of them had Teilhard's detailed sense of paleontology, geology, and cosmology.

Could you put that into plain language. What exactly did he see?

He saw that you can't have a material universe without a psychic dimension, which gives it intelligibility. That's the difficulty with people who interpret the genetic code and think they've solved something. They may know how to manipulate a tree genetically, for example, but they don't understand the unifying principle that enables that tree to function with such complexity—to send down roots, to create a trunk and branches, to carry on its manifold functioning. So with the universe itself. It obviously has an intelligibility.

Do you mean an intelligence?

Well, first we're aware of an intelligibility—we can know it. If we can know it, it must have a basic psychic structure, which also has an active consciousness dimension. Trees, atoms, animals—all have their own consciousness. They also have their own language and their own voice. These are different from human consciousness and human language, yet they're intelligible. That's why children and animals understand each other. We're multilingual in that sense. We are born with a certain Earth literacy, an ability to read the language of the natural world, but we don't develop it.

In earlier Christian times they talked about the two books, the book of nature and the book of the Bible. Ever since the development of printing in the 15th century, the written book has come to predominate, and we've lost the book of nature. In fact, every time we destroy a species, we tear out and burn another whole library of revelation.

This reminds me of the I-thou relationship that Martin Buber talks about, in which everything is perceived as subject rather than object, as a thou, with its own mystery and divinity, rather than as some inanimate it.

Exactly. Everything is subject. We can commune with subject in our relationship with the sun, moon, and stars. That's why a planet like Venus was given such a beautiful name and such beautiful qualities. The ancients had a subject-subject rapport with the natural world. It wasn't just a set of figures in a scientific formula.

I think of Meister Eckhart's "The eye with which I see God is the eye with which God sees me." A true subject-to-subject relationship.

That's where the scientist misses the point and doesn't understand the mystical dimension behind the scientific formula.

Say a little more.

The scientific formula has a number of components, but what binds them together and gives them meaning is the mythic, mystical dimension behind everything. The universe is a functional unity; if you vary any one thing, you vary the whole. Part and whole are identical.

One of the reasons we're destroying the planet is that it has lost its sacred dimension for us. The planet as given to us by science is a physical reality essentially meaningless in itself. It's a resource for our physical activity. It can't be sacralized because it doesn't have subjectivity in our eyes.

We've lost our reverence for trees, for example. No wonder we cut them down. If we can't utilize them, we don't think they have any value. Progress lies in conquering the natural world. The less we're associated with nature, the greater the progress. In the secular world view, nature is sacralized by use and by being turned into junk. The highest achievement of a forest is to be turned into paper pulp or lumber for houses.

This view seems to be based on the Christian tradition, with its hierarchy or "great chain of being" that puts human beings at the top.

Yes, our religious tradition is largely responsible for this alienation, for several reasons. First of all, we've constellated a divine presence in some transcendent reality and established a covenant with it. The idea that a covenant relationship is an ideal way of relating with the divine is crazy.

Say more about the difficulties of the covenant relationship.

A covenant is a legal contract. Whereas if the divine is understood as a pervasive presence in the universe, there's a sense of intimacy. We encounter the divine in everything—in the dawn, in the sunset, in growing things, flowers, trees, animals.

That's the I-thou relationship again.

Yes, and it's also where the divine is appreciated in its nurturing aspect, where the mother deities dominate. A transcendent deity is inevitably a masculine figure. With a covenant relationship you're already in trouble. The

Prophets were denouncing the legalism within the tradition even in Old Testament times. They criticized the overemphasis on sacrifice and ritual at the expense of mercy and compassion. But they didn't address the problem of the human-Earth relation. So I like to phrase the First Commandment this way: "I am the Lord thy God, thou shalt not have an Earth mother before me."

This attitude sets the sacred outside the natural world.

That's right, it desacralizes it. The next thing the Christian tradition does is to establish human beings, and even a special segment of humans, as a spiritual elite, over against the rest of creation, which is considered nonspiritual. We say, "Don't treat humans like things." I say, "Don't treat things like things, because there is no such thing as a thing." The human is so arrogant. Third, Christianity stresses the redemption experience—the important thing is to be redeemed out of this world.

This complex of qualities represents what I call the dark side of the Christian religious tradition. Of course, scripture scholars are always trying to glorify the Bible. Someone said, I think it was Matthew Fox, that the Bible is the most overrated book in the world. What I say is that we should put the Bible on the shelf for 20 years until we learn to read the revelation of the natural world.

Let's get back to the three ways you were influenced by Teilhard.

Well, the first, as I've said, is being able to tell the story of the psychospiritual dimension of the universe. The second is identifying our personal human story with the story of the universe. Our personal being is our microphase self, and the universe is our macrophase self. We also have a community self, an Earth self. In other words, we're not ourselves without everything else. It took billions of years to create the human hand; it couldn't have been created earlier or later and still be this same hand. The supernova explosions, the shaping of the planet Earth, all were necessary. People sometimes ask, Why is the universe as big or as old as it is? Because it took that long to create the conditions for life and consciousness as we know them.

In other words, we are the fruit of an incredibly long and complex process.

Articulated by the human. This is where Teilhard is very clear: The human is that being in whom the universe reflects on itself in a special mode of conscious self-awareness. It's not that we know the universe; the universe knows itself through us.

So we have a special function to play.

Very special. Many people nowadays object to the notion that humans are special. They claim that we don't belong to a hierarchy of beings and that all beings are in fact equal.

Deep ecologists take that position, for example.

Yes. My answer is, I don't do away with hierarchy, I universalize it. I don't believe that everything is equally important. Everything is important in its own way; everything is at the top of the hierarchy in its own way. When it comes to flying, the bird is on top. When it comes to swimming, the fish is on top. When it comes to making apples, the apple tree. When it comes to reflective thought, the humans. Each thing has its own distinct perfection. Now it's true that the importance of things is relative to the whole. But to say one thing is equal to another implies that one of them is unnecessary. There's no need for me if somebody else has all the qualities I have.

So equality isn't an appropriate way to talk about it. Each thing is unique.

Absolutely. The Middle Ages had a wonderful expression: "The individual is ineffable." That's why there's no science of the individual. Science deals with statistical averages, not with the reality of anything. It can tell you an awful lot about illness or medicine in general, but the specific way in which this illness is affecting a particular individual is extremely complex and mysterious.

Then the third point Teilhard made was to shift the religious issue from redemption to creation. The Western world is so overwhelmed by the Biblical experience that its primary spiritual concern has been redemption.

In other words, to be redeemed out of the world, to be saved from the dilemma we are incarnated into.

Almost all the prayers in the Catholic missal are for achieving some form of relief from the difficulties of time. In baptism, the child achieves a special Christian relationship with the divine and becomes a member of a religious community. But nothing is mentioned about its rapport with the natural world. When I do a baptism, I use, in addition to the baptismal ritual that's generally prescribed, the Omaha [Native American] ritual for introducing a child to the universe. Sun, moon, stars, the rains and storms, the grasses and insects—all of the natural world is involved, and the child is presented to the four directions as a new being who has entered into the vast community and whose welfare depends on the assistance of the total universe.

It's a kind of bonding.

Exactly, a bonding of the child to the larger community to which it belongs. But there is almost no awareness of this in the Christian tradition. The same thing with the Apostle's Creed: "I believe in God the father almighty, creator of heaven and earth and in Jesus Christ his only son" and so forth. It slides over the creation and goes on to a long articulation of redemption.

What does the creation emphasis offer that the redemption emphasis doesn't?

The creation emphasis focuses on the universe itself, its inner structures, its sacred dimension, its deeper mysteries. We come to a sense of the divine through the beauty of the natural world. To the degree that the beauty of the world is diminished, our sense of the divine is diminished as well. If we lived on the moon, our sense of the divine would reflect the lunar landscape. Our imagination would be as empty as the moon, our sensitivities as dull, and we would have practically no intellectual life. Insofar as the natural world is diminished, our inner world is diminished in proportion.

Say a little more about that.

It's so obvious. How are you going to have poetry or write music on the moon? How are you going to have any of the thoughts that come to our mind here on the planet Earth? You would have only desolate experience.

Because the richness of our inner life comes from our experience of the richness of the planet.

The inner world has to be constantly nourished by the outer world. With what we are doing to the outer world now, we are damaging our psychic structure as well as reducing our resources. Take earthquakes and hurricanes, for example. Though they may be devastating in one way, they provide enormous enrichment of our psychic experience, because they dramatically deepen our sense of the awesomeness of things. They also reveal to us quite vividly that with all our science, we're not in charge. After the big San Francisco earthquake several years ago, a gathering of scientific experts concluded that there was a 50 percent chance of another serious earthquake happening within the next 30 years. Can you imagine! With all their scientific knowledge!

You talked earlier about the special role humans play as a means for the universe to be conscious of itself. What exactly is our role right now, in this moment of history?

Our role is to establish a mutually enhancing rapport with the natural world. It's a movement from anthropocentrism to biocentrism. Our only hope is to join in the ever-renewing processes of nature. The industrial world can't renew itself: bridges, roads, machines disintegrate. It's a one-way process. We can bolster them, but the industrial world is doomed; it's falling to pieces.

Because resources are limited?

For three reasons. Firts of all, when we erected the industrial infrastructures of our society, we had enormous psychic energy. We had great hope, and people worked for very little. Now we want to be paid for every last bit of effort we put in, and we don't have the same expectations, because we're not sure it's all worthwhile. And the infrastructures are breaking up faster than we can repair them.

Second, it would cost a hundred times more to rebuild those infrastructures than it took to put them up in the first place. We don't have anywhere near the resources. It would cost a trillion dollars just to begin to repair the bridges, the water and power systems, the schools and public buildings, which are deteriorating rapidly throughout the country.

Third, the natural resources are not so abundant. At a certain order of magnitude it might be manageable. For example, roads in some parts of the country might last longer than in others, but generally they break up faster than we can repair them. Look at the automobile industry—millions of tires and batteries are thrown away each year. The junk continues to pile up. There are 400 million automobiles in the world now, and there will be 600 million by the end of this century.

What do we do, then, with the industrial and technological infrastructure?

Close it down.

And then?

Begin community life, with a new emphasis on basic crafts and community gardens. Begin with a new sense of scale, a new sense of the relationship between where we live and where we work, so we don't have the enormous congestion of our big cities. Take care of our wetlands, our forests, our rivers, rather than abusing them.

Even in a place like New York City, certain areas within my memory were farms, and New Jersey was the wonderful Garden State. Now all that is paved over, damaged, exploited.

What I'm suggesting is not impossible. People like Wes Jackson, John and Nancy Todd, the folks at the Rodale Institute, and many others have begun to articulate ways in which we can begin to make sense out of our existence. But right now we're devastating not only this continent, but countries all over the world. In fact, we're surviving by plundering the rest of the planet. In a recent year, something like $37 billion more in resources went from the Third World to the First World than vice versa. It's like taking a blood transfusion from the patient to the doctor.

Our economics are totally illusory for one simple reason—they don't factor in the Earth equation. All human corporations are subsidiaries of the Earth corporation. If the GNP goes up and the GEP (gross Earth product) goes down, there will be no future. The least we can do is to recognize and identify the nature of the issue, and then begin this process of adaptation. It's not nearly as impossible or as impractical as people think.

What about technology? Is there appropriate technology?

Obviously, because nature itself is a technology. The rain is an elaborate engineering feat for taking all the water into the sky and pouring it down over the continents. We need to develop human technology that is integral with earth technology.

But appropriate technology isn't really the big issue. What is most important is the willingness to accept the human situation. Our difficulties arise from the fact that we're not willing to accept the conditions under which life is granted to us. We fight them, we try to turn night into day and day into night, winter into summer and summer into winter, but ultimately we're playing a losing game. We can exploit the planet for a while, drive up the GNP at the expense of the GEP, but the consequences are inevitable. We have to accept existence at the human level under the conditions that brought us into being.

This is what the American Indians would call walking in balance.

Walking in balance, walking in harmony, and walking in the presence of a bountiful world.

How did you arrive at the title of your book, Dream of the Earth*?*

I look upon the Earth as part of a stupendous imaginative process that has produced all the different varieties of flowers, marine life, trees, birds—such uncounted profusion, all integral with each other.

A traditionally religious person within the Judeo-Christian tradition might call it God's imagination.

That's right. But whatever the source, it has fantastic shaping powers. The great geneticist Dobzhansky insisted that the universe is not simply random, nor is it predetermined, it's creative. That's a very important word. So with the planet Earth—anything that is creative has an imaginative dimension. Whereas St. John says, "In the beginning was the word," the logos or the intelligible origin of things, and from this everything comes, I suggest we say, "In the beginning was the dream, the dream was with God, the dream was God, and through the dream were all things made." Because in dreams the imagination is functioning most freely; we can imagine things in our dreams we couldn't possibly figure out.

This imaginative process is enormously productive, but it's uncontrollable. Rather than trying to control it, we need to enter into the play of things—the dream, the play, the dance, the ritual. In India it's called the dance of Shiva. We're invited to join in this dance, but we refuse.

We've lost our attunement to the natural world.

Yes, and this attunement is what we need to regain.

John Robbins

John Robbins's journey from rich kid to rebel to vegetarian crusader is the kind that myths are made of. The title of the story might be something like this: Heir to Ice Cream Empire Takes On the Great American Food Machine. Groomed from childhood to succeed his father as head of Baskin-Robbins, Robbins declined the family fortune at age 20 because, as he says quite simply, "my heart wasn't in it." A lengthy personal and spiritual odyssey followed, including years of meditation, numerous trips to India, and stints as a yoga teacher, growth center founder, and workshop leader. Yet always, Robbins remained troubled by the false promise of instant happiness purveyed by his father's company. Now, more than two decades later, he has written a book that shakes the animal foods industry to its very foundations.

What prompted the boyishly handsome Robbins, who lives with his wife and teenage son in Santa Cruz, California, to spend three years researching the atrocities of factory farming? "I started having a series of dreams in which a giant cow appeared to me," he explains. "Then I saw a giant pig. And they would say things to me, powerful things about life and our relationship to them and to the natural world. Finally I received a very clear message that said, 'You are to write this book. You will be guided the entire way. It's not to be preachy, it's not to charm or coerce people, it's just to let the truth be known.'"

The result, *Diet for a New America*, is an eloquent, meticulously documented indictment of the meat, poultry, and dairy industries—so eloquent, in fact, that it was nominated for a Pulitzer Prize in nonfiction. Robbins himself, who stopped eating meat shortly after leaving home, had experimented with "just about every dietary regime that came down the pike." It was not until a friend and yoga teacher suggested that he give up dairy products as well (and become a pure vegetarian) that he began giving serious consideration to all the profound ramifications of eating animal products.

"I had come to take matters of diet somewhat lightly, feeling that the kind of person you are is more important than what you eat," says Robbins. "Watching so many people seek their health, salvation, and freedom through eating or not eating various foods, I had developed a certain sense of humor about the whole process. Yet, in writing *Diet for a New America*, I found a wealth of evidence suggesting that the eating habits that support human health have social and environmental benefits too."

In addition to practicing as a bodyworker and psychotherapist, Robbins is founder and president of EarthSave Foundation, an organization devoted to letting people know how "human health, well-being, and survival are inextricably interwoven with the fate of all forms of life on Earth." Among the foundation's projects are a film, videotape, and audio-cassettes based on the book, as well as nutritional and environmental education materials for schools, to replace those disseminated by the animal foods industry.

John Robbins

Diet for a New America

One of the things that impressed me most about your book was its compassion. One could so easily be tempted to be judgmental of people who are cruel to animals. But I sense throughout the book a lack of judgment and a compassionate attitude, not only toward the animals but toward the people who exploit them.

Thank you. I think it's so important to embody compassion, especially when it's most difficult. It's easy to love someone who makes you feel good. But it's wonderfully freeing to love someone who doesn't seem to deserve it.

My life has been a series of opportunities to ask myself the question "What does it mean to love your enemy?" Obviously it doesn't mean placating them or condoning what they do. We have a responsibility to protest and expose certain things. Generally, our anger is telling us something. Maybe we need to break down a wall that's arisen between people, or raise the energy or consciousness of a situation. The trouble is, we've only had destructive models of anger. We hardly know how to use our anger in the loving service of others.

So you're not advocating a kind of "idiot compassion."

Not at all. Idiot compassion is naive. It gets us nowhere and actually makes us intensely vulnerable to exploitation.

In writing the book, I wanted to reach a broad audience, so I had to do a lot of careful research. This research took me to some ghastly places where I saw and heard and smelled some horrible things that I was helpless to do anything about. I had to struggle to keep my heart open, to remain conscious and not go emotionally and psychically numb.

One form this psychic numbing would take was anger. I could sense that the anger was a way of protecting myself, a way of pulling away from an immediate and open and available connection to what was happening. It made me feel strong and invulnerable in a certain way, but it also distanced me.

The anger burned in me like a fire. At first I didn't know what to do with it. But I found that, if I didn't react against it or jump to any conclusions and stayed what I call "Christ-centered," it had its own wisdom and intelligence. It would change into a deep feeling of caring, which then gave me a clearer sense of what I wanted to see changed and what I could do about it.

In the Tibetan Buddhist tradition, the positive side of anger is a kind of decisive clarity that cuts through all obstacles. Your book strikes a wonderful balance between, on the one hand, stories that touch the heart (and make a strong case just in the telling) and, on the other hand, some precise, well-documented, and persuasive arguments.

One of the most important things I learned while researching and writing the book is that what serves us serves others, too. Often in our lives it seems that we have to compromise what we believe in and have to choose between the lesser of two evils. We're constantly faced with the moral ambiguity of our existence. What I found with food choices is that we don't have to make any trade-offs: The most health-supporting choices for us personally are also the best for the environment, the most compassionate, and the best for the economy. It's remarkable how many spokes radiate from the same central hub.

Five years ago, if you had asked me what I felt about food choices and spirituality, I probably would have said that a spiritual person is someone who can adapt to any situation, can transform any vibration, can maintain their integrity and be a dynamic embodiment of the godliness within under any circumstances.

Both Sufis and Zen Buddhists would probably agree with that.

Yes. But I've become aware that our spiritual presence also requires that we be aware of what we're doing and of the impact we're having on the world and our fellow beings. Spirituality that isn't socially responsible is sterile.

Living in these times, we can't help but participate in great tides of social change. One hundred fifty years ago slavery was legal in this country. Eighty years ago women couldn't vote. Today we have the kind of unconsciousness about how animals are treated in routine meat production that our ancestors had about the issue of slavery 200 years ago. How, we ask now, could people of the quality of Jefferson and Washington have kept slaves? Our grandchildren will look back and wonder how otherwise good people like us could have tolerated such cruel treatment of animals.

Why do you think vegetarianism and the animal rights movement are so important?

The development of compassion, health, and sanity in the human being is indispensable for our evolution. Without it we won't survive. And I'm not advocating a puritan, "never-eat-meat-under-any-circumstances" attitude. But any conscious and sensitive person would find today's factory farms appalling and unacceptable.

One of the spokes in this "wheel" you've described, then, is that if we eat food that comes from factory farms, we are in fact supporting the systematic torture of billions of animals.

Yes. The sad thing is that otherwise humane and moral people justify this brutality by saying it has always been done. Certainly animals have been treated cruelly down through the ages. In fact, one cynic has said that the chief characteristic of humanity throughout history has been our inhumanity. But the cruelty has never been institutionalized and mass-produced before. And never has the cold expertise of technology, in the guise of today's factory-farming methods and the pharmaceutical industry, been so deeply involved.

With drugs you can now keep an animal alive under conditions where before it would have died of stress. Animals raised in factory farms (and this includes feedlot cattle, 99.9 percent of all chickens, both broilers and laying hens, and just about all our pigs and veal calves) are fed a steady stream of dangerous drugs. Most are given daily doses of antibiotics as part of their normal feed. This practice breeds antibiotic-resistant bacteria in their intestines and stomachs, which then become part of our bacteriological environment. Our wonder-drug antibiotics are losing their power to heal and are, as a consequence, being vastly overprescribed in humans. Staph infections used to be treatable by penicillin; now 90 percent of them are resistant. Pneumonia and other bacterial diseases are much harder to treat than they used to be.

Not to speak of the drugs we ingest when we eat the meat, eggs, or milk of these animals.

That's another thing I found out about in great detail. We like to think we're protected, but we're not. The violet dye used by the FDA to stamp meat "U.S. number one" finally had to be pulled off the market because it was carcinogenic. Can you imagine? The violet dye! The FDA can't protect the food supply from these drugs. They're so expensive to test for that the tests are hardly being carried out at all. The number of dangerous drugs used in the animal products industry today is astonishing.

For example, chloramphenicol was marketed for years as a powerful antibiotic for animal use. It also causes, in a small but significant percentage of human beings, a fatal disease called aplastic anemia. There's no way to know in advance who is going to succumb. The company that made the drug knew about this, yet they continued to deny it for years.

Finally the whole thing came to light, and the use of chloramphenicol was declared illegal except in extremely rare circumstances, when no other antibiotic will do and it's a life-threatening situation. Incredibly minute amounts can kill susceptible people. Yet I've seen it used regularly on veal calves. There's no way that a person who died from it, or whose system was thrown out of kilter by it, would know where it came from.

Another really bad instance is the implantation of hormones in cattle, sometimes in dairy cows. If a pregnant woman drinks cow's milk, it is quite possible that without knowing it she's taking in estrogens. If there's a young male in her womb, that young boy is going to be affected in a serious way. A lot of cases of premature puberty (not to mention cancer) have been directly traced to the hormones in beef and dairy cattle.

Yes, I was terribly disturbed by studies done in Puerto Rico, where the use of hormones is not as well regulated as in the States. Little girls fed cow's milk and chicken laced with hormones were developing breasts at the age of five.

Yes, and pubic hair at age two and three. Even in this country, with our better but still woefully inadequate system of public health controls, the age of onset of menstruation in women has been going steadily down. It's dropped over four years in the last 150 years. Children are growing into puberty earlier and earlier, in such an abrupt and shocking way that it throws their whole system out of balance. They don't have the natural time to develop their sexual identity. A lot of factors contribute to this, but on a biochemical level it's directly traceable to two things: the excessive fats in the American diet—particularly animal fats—and the hormone residues carried in those fats.

A person who is studying yoga or some other psycho-spiritual discipline and wants to become more peaceful and alive really needs to consider the spiritual and moral implications of their food choices. The standard yogic diet is lacto-vegetarian, which means that it includes milk products. But today's dairy products are a far cry indeed from the milk, butter, and cheese of the "contented cows" of yesteryear. The ads for dairy products make it all look so natural and wholesome that you would never suspect how much misery is involved. Yet sensitive people start to pick it up and manifest it.

What is the misery in milk, besides the hormones?

The animals in most dairies are confined to a very small space. They can't move around, and many live their whole lives on slotted stainless steel floors that destroy their hooves and carriage. They've also been bred to have gigantic udders. If their babies were to suckle on them, their udders would probably be damaged. That's another part of the misery: Their children are taken away. They never get to nurse their calves. Instead they're hooked up to electronic milking machines.

So through the milk we're getting hormones produced by a cow undergoing intense stress and suffering, and we're ingesting that suffering through the milk.

Exactly. Every breast-feeding mother learns that when she's in a good mood her baby relaxes, and when she's in a bad mood the baby spits up. The milk carries how she feels, just as her touch does. If an infant is not responding well to breast milk, a sensitive physician will first look at the mother's overall situation to make sure she's relaxed and at ease with herself, so that she can bond more fully and her milk will express that bonding and caring. Well, today's cow's milk comes from tormented animals. And those of us who eat products made from that milk are taking on their suffering.

Another aspect of the misery in milk is that male calves born to dairy cows can't be made into milk machines, so they're made into veal. Veal is not a special breed of calf; veal calves are male dairy calves that are fed government surplus dried skim milk powder mixed with petroleum products and the most incredible array of chemicals you could imagine. Of all the factory-farm atrocities, veal calf treatment is the worst. They're taken at birth and crammed into a crate about the size of the trunk of your car, chained at the neck, and left there in the dark. These are babies. Their umbilical cords are often still attached. They can't assume their normal sleeping posture, can't lick themselves, are isolated from any contact with other calves, and they're never allowed to take a single step. Twice a day the lights are turned on so they can be fed a gruel that is deliberately designed to produce anemia; it keeps their flesh a pinkish white. Since they're not permitted to move, their muscles never develop. The result is the "tender, delicate" veal so highly prized in gourmet restaurants. This hideously cruel treatment is part and parcel of today's dairy industry.

These are some pretty powerful reasons for not eating dairy products. But what about calcium? An article on osteoporosis in a recent issue of Yoga Journal *[March-April 1988] recommends dairy products as the best dietary source of calcium.*

Yes, I read that article. The exercise section is excellent, and the author is obviously a very knowledgeable and sophisticated person. But her discussion of the nutritional aspects of osteoporosis misses one point (and I'm fully prepared to document this from the literature). She claims that you need 1500 milligrams of calcium per day to protect against osteoporosis—and that may be true for postmenopausal women. But the rest of us need 1500 milligrams *only* if we are eating a lot of protein, particularly animal protein.

Because animal protein is high in phosphorous?

Three reasons: first, because it's high in phosphorous; second, because it's acid-forming and your body needs extra calcium to buffer the acidity (calcium is very alkaline); and third, because the protein leaches calcium out of the bones and into the urinary system. The biggest argument against excessive protein, as far as I'm concerned, is what it does to your calcium balance. The largest study ever done on osteoporosis and diet was conducted at Michigan State and a number of other major universities and written up in the *Journal of Clinical Nutrition* several years ago. What they found was that the average 65-year-old meat-eating woman in the United States has lost 35 percent of her bone density. Thirty-five percent of her skeleton is gone! Her bones may be the same size outwardly, but the insides have become porous and fragile and prone to fracture.

The average 65-year-old lacto-ovo-vegetarian woman, in comparison, has lost 18 percent. One-half as much. And it's quite probable that the bone loss in women who followed a pure vegetarian diet would be significantly less than that. Vegetarian women have far stronger bones, far fewer fractures, and if they do break a bone they heal much more quickly. They are much more athletic and active as they age, and they retain their height—which is not just an aesthetic concern but has important health implications as well. And osteoporosis is almost entirely preventable without calcium supplements or dairy products, as long as you don't eat meat, overconsume other proteins, or fail to exercise.

The National Dairy Council, which of course touts dairy products as a solution to osteoporosis, has commissioned a number of studies to try to prove that dairy products are the answer. But the studies keep showing something different. One of the largest, funded by the Dairy Council itself, was conducted in England and published in the *American Journal of Clinical Nutrition.* For a year, a group of women drank three eight-ounce glasses of low-fat milk a day, in addition to their regular diet. The control group received no extra milk. The two groups were very carefully monitored for a full year, so the researchers knew what everyone was eating, whether they were taking any calcium supplements, what their histories were, and so on. They made allowances for all the variables that could conceivably distort the findings. They regularly monitored the urine and blood levels for calcium. What they found was that the women who took the extra milk derived no benefit to their bone density. And the researchers knew why: Any possible advantage from the extra calcium was offset by the additional protein from the low-fat milk.

Osteoporosis is a complex disease with many factors, but the most important by far is protein consumption. That's why Bantu women, who get only one-quarter our supposed "minimum daily requirement" of calcium, never get osteoporosis, even though they bear many children and breast-feed them for two years each. They don't overconsume protein, particularly animal protein, so their calcium balance stays in line. They seldom break a bone and rarely lose a tooth. But when Bantu women switch to a meat-centered diet, their osteoporosis rates rival ours.

Native Eskimos are another story. They have the highest calcium intake of any people in the world. If osteoporosis were a calcium-deficiency disease, it would be unheard of among the Eskimos. But their diet is also the highest in protein, and so they have one of the highest osteoporosis rates in the world.

Aside from the health issue, what are some of the ecological and political ramifications of eating meat? Why not eat range-fed, organically raised beef, for example? These animals are well treated, no hormones or pesticides are used, and if we eat it in small quantities we're not getting too much protein.

The first issue that comes to mind is world hunger. We all know that millions of people are hungry right now, but it's so painful to keep this in mind that most of us don't know the exact numbers. So we probably don't know that the children who die of starvation each day would fill 35 jumbo jets. If a 747 crashed killing all its occupants, it would make world headlines. If the unfortunate plane were filled with children, there would be a Congressional investigation. But the equivalent of thirty-five 747s filled with children are dying of starvation every day!

The pain of that knowledge is so intense that we have to find ways of dealing with it. The tried and true way in our culture is denial—just go unconscious about it and block it out. I'm sure most of your readers aren't satisfied in the slightest with that response and are looking for a way of doing what they can within the significant limits of their situation.

Most people don't realize to what extent their eating habits affect world hunger. If the American people were to reduce their consumption of meat by 10 percent, it would free up enough grain to feed adequately every one of the 60 million people who will otherwise die of starvation this year. The amount of grain it takes to feed 100 cattle would feed 2,000 people.

It's amazing how much waste is involved in a meat-based diet. An acre of land will produce 20,000 pounds of potatoes; the same acre of land will produce only 165 pounds of beef. Which do you suppose provides more food for a starving world?

The reason this wastefulness doesn't show up at the cash register is that these industries are so heavily subsidized. For example, if the cattle industry had to pay for their water what the average person pays, the price of ground beef would be 35 dollars a pound. The amount of water it takes to raise a thousand-pound steer would float a destroyer. In fact, over half the water consumed in the United States is consumed by the cattle industry. Half the water! A lot of it is used to wash away the manure and to water the crops that are fed to the cows.

Not only do the cattlemen use all that water, they pollute what's left at a staggering rate. The meat industry single-handedly accounts for more than three times as much harmful organic waste water pollution as the rest of the nation's industries combined. A typical feedlot accumulates more excrement than the entire city of San Francisco. But it's all in one place, it would be extremely expensive to return it to the earth, and they rarely recycle it. So it ends up in our streams and rivers, setting off a whole chain of adverse ecological reactions that are destroying our waterways.

Also, it takes enormous energy to get the meat on the table—to grow all that extra grain, to transport it to the feedlots, to provide heat for the animals (which isn't always done), to clean up after them, to slaughter them and refrigerate the meat and ship it to market. The meat industry uses more energy than any other industry. Actually, the feedlots and the factory farms are designed to use energy instead of human labor. They are very poor providers of jobs, as poor as any industry in the country. They are capital- and energy-intensive. The average factory poultry operation, for example, houses 90,000 chickens, with only a few employees to run the whole thing. It's all done by machines, conveyor belts, and electricity.

So the word "factory farm" means just that.

That's right. They do everything they can to eliminate human involvement. For one thing, human beings can't stand the conditions. They go crazy. Slaughterhouses have the highest employee turnover rate of any occupation in the country. They are places of tremendous pain and suffering. And the men and women who work there are carrying a burden for the rest of us. That's why I feel so much compassion for them. They're doing it for us. They've grown such a thick callous over their hearts because they are the embodiment of our denial. To the degree that we can shift our country to a better and more conscious way of eating, we can welcome these people back to meaningful jobs and to kinship with life. They've born the brunt of our insensitivity, our psychic numbing, and our short-sighted understanding of what food is.

They're like the soldiers on the front line, fighting a war for the rest of us.

Right. And even if we buy organically fed meat, it's still slaughtered, quite probably under the same inhumane conditions. I don't say you have to be a vegetarian to care about animals, to want to be healthy and want your life to be a statement of higher values. But I do believe that the more vegetarian and the more natural you can become, the less polluted your body's going to be, the clearer your mind, and the less you're going to be supporting with your life the activities that are destroying our planet.

What are some of the other environmental ramifications?

Well, take deforestation. The deforestation in this country is so rapid and so severe that at our current rates, if we don't change, there won't be a single tree left in 50 years. Most of that, we normally think, comes from urban development and paper products. But the truth is that six times more deforestation in this country is caused by the cattle industry than by urban expansion.

And the trees used for paper are actually renewed.

Yes, the better companies take care of their tree crops. But the cattlemen come in, lease land from the Bureau of Land Management, and clearcut the forests. They graze their cattle, destroying the eco-system, and then move on to the next piece of land. They don't own it, so they don't care. Meanwhile the forests are cut down, and the soil is eroded.

The cattle industry is also responsible for a tremendous amount of soil erosion for another reason: We're having to farm more and more of our marginal lands—and even our better lands with an unprecedented degree of rapacity, using pesticides and chemical fertilizers—because we have to force production beyond all natural limits in order to grow enough food for our livestock. We use poisons like there's no tomorrow—and if we keep using them, there won't be.

So, by your statistics, it takes much less land to grow crops directly for human consumption.

To supply food for a year to a person eating a meat-centered diet requires 3 1/4 acres. For a lacto-ovo-vegetarian, it takes half an acre, and for a pure vegetarian only a quarter acre.

Another environmental catastrophe the cattlemen are involved in is the destruction of the rainforests. The Rainforest Action Network's boycott of Burger King forced them to stop using rainforest meat in their continental U.S. outlets. But they continue to use it in their international outlets, and the beef industry as a whole continues to force the clearing of the forests in Central America, just as they do here, grazing the cattle and turning the world's richest ecological habitats into deserts.

The rainforests not only provide much of the world's oxygen, they are home to 90 percent of the world's species of animal and plant life. We're destroying one species per hour now—not just a representative of a species, but an entire species! Once it's gone, it's gone forever. How many billion years did it take for that species to evolve in its own niche, its own ecosystem? To me this is where spirituality, environmentalism, and eating habits all come together. You don't even have to be particularly spiritual to be appalled by this. Cornell economists who studied the matter in great depth have estimated that every person who switches to a strictly vegetarian diet saves an acre of trees a year.

If 10 million people became vegetarians, that would be 10 million acres. That's an enormous amount of land.

It's amazing how much is to be gained by switching to a more vegetarian diet. There isn't a single environmental issue I'm aware of that wouldn't be significantly and positively affected. Even the ozone layer is involved. The feedlots give off enormous amounts of methane, as do the termites that devour what remains of a forest after it has been clearcut. And this methane apparently interferes with the ozone layer. A switch to a more vegetarian diet would also mean we could eliminate our terrible overuse of nitrogenous fertilizers, which also contribute to ozone layer damage. Not to mention unhooking from the pesticides and other artificial fertilizers that are doing so much to destroy the biosphere.

Let's turn to the title of your book, Diet for a New America. *Back in 1971, Frances Moore Lappe wrote* Diet for a Small Planet, *in which she makes a very persuasive case for giving up meat. But she also warns that if we eat a lacto-vegetarian diet, we need to combine our proteins in certain ways in order to get enough. Now you've been warning about the dangers of eating too much protein. What's the scoop? If we're going to do without meat, dairy products, chicken, fish, and eggs, are we going to be able to get enough protein?*

You're right about what Frances Moore Lappe wrote in the original edition of *Diet for a Small Planet.* But she republished the book in 1976 and again in 1981, each time bringing it up to date with what she had learned since. In both revised editions, particularly in the later one, she totally repudiates the idea that we need to combine proteins. This is remarkable: The woman who introduced protein-combining to the world and became famous as a result now tells us that it is totally unnecessary.

Most people still assume that to get enough protein without meat, you have to eat dairy products and be careful, á la Lappe's book in its original form. But all the protein research in even the most conservative medical and nutritional literature over the last 10 or 15 years indicates that you'd have to work at *not* getting enough protein, given a diet of basic, natural foods. In fact, people with kidney problems, who must restrict their protein intake, find it difficult to do.

I'm not asking people to take my word for it; they can refer to the original studies. It's all documented in my book—who did what, and where, and why the study was important, and exactly what the methodology was and what conclusions they came to. There has been a revolution in the last 10 or 15 years in our understanding of protein and how much we need. The medical information speaks with one voice. We don't have to worry about getting enough; we'd be better off worrying about getting too much. Yet the fear of not getting enough protein has been systematically instilled in us by the lobbying efforts of the companies that sell high-protein foods.

I asked the American Heart Association why they advise people to cut down on their meat, rather than to eliminate it, when an editorial in the *Journal of the American Medical Association* said that 97 percent of our heart attacks could be prevented by a vegetarian diet. I also asked clinicians why they tell potential osteoporosis sufferers to drink more milk, rather than to drop the excess protein. In each case, the reasoning was the same. "Look," they argued, "if we prescribe a sick patient a medication that he's not going to take because it's unpalatable or too expensive, we've failed in our responsibility to him. We have to find something the patient will take. Now, we're talking to the American public, and the American public is not motivated to change their eating habits."

Yes. Food is an incredibly emotional issue. People associate food with nurturing, with their upbringing, with their childhood. And the food they ate when they were children is the food that gives them satisfaction.

Dick Gregory said the hardest thing he had to deal with when he started changing his diet was the nagging thought, "Does this mean mama was wrong?"

We're creatures of habit. And in our lives today we're being asked to change a lot of those habits. Each of us has a choice of either doing the automatic, habitual thing or else applying awareness and intelligence to find out what is truly called for from us. Doing the automatic and habitual thing not only keeps us asleep, it will ultimately destroy our world.

We are being asked to question our very roots, psychologically and emotionally, so that we can discover who we actually are. Spiritual teachers have always told us, "Find out who you are. Don't take other people's word for it. Access your own being and find out what you really want to do. Live with integrity. Trust yourself." But many people say, "How can I trust myself? I've done so many crazy things." The spiritual teachers reply, "Try it and see. Find out what you can trust in yourself by trying different things. Experiment. Explore." When we do that, we find that some of the alternatives are blind alleys, and others are life affirming, giving us access to our creativity, our joy, our true health, and our spiritual fulfillment. Then we're on to something we can build our lives around.

And we can't find that unless we experiment, unless we let go of the old and invite the new.

Exactly. In my book I'm inviting people to give it a try. I'm not saying you need to be a vegetarian, though you might decide it's a good idea, once you've seen what's being done to the animals, what's in the food, and what we know about the health and environmental consequences of eating animal products. Undertake a journey on your own behalf and on behalf of all life. It may be selfish in that you'll feel better. But it isn't selfish in the narrow sense, because it also involves and gives life to so many of the values you really hold dear.

It's thrilling to realize that what serves you serves others too. The most socially responsible and "politically correct" way of eating is also the healthiest, the most economical, the kindest, and the most liberating. Finding that out, which is a process that each of us must go through individually, has been one of the great joys of my life, because, in seeing that, I've discovered a pattern operating in our lives and in the natural world—call it the law of God, or cosmic law, or universal intelligence.

We're not put here to fight with each other. There is enough to go around. What is best for me is best for you. I don't have to ignore your needs or shut out the Third World or ethnic minorities or the animals or the environment in order to get my needs met. I don't have to build my identity on competition. As a matter of fact, my beingness grows its deepest roots into the fertility of the universe just by taking this adventure of living with a heart open equally to my own needs and the needs of others.

I think there's also a mythic component to this attachment to meat. You know, the American myth of the cowboy and steak and potatoes, the myth that a real man eats meat.

Frances Lappe called it the Great American Steak Religion, and it has been deeply ingrained in us by the food lobbies we've been talking about. The company my father founded has been a foremost proponent of the ice cream part of that myth.

But there's a deeper myth in our psyches. I know because magnificent cows and other animals came into my dream life and spoke to me from a profound level of numinosity. The deeper American dream is of a society at peace with its conscience, living in harmony with all life forms, finding joy in making a conscious contribution to the web of life. But even the standard American dream has something to offer. The society I'm talking about is one where people can be free to differ.

Every step we take out of our deepest conscience helps bring a collective conscience to life. Every step we take out of our caring, our heart, our dedication to truth helps, because we are a shared consciousness, we are parts of the same body. It sends a signal out through the Earth's bloodstream, through the neural connections of the human mind, that it's possible to live together without hunger, without conflict, without cruelty toward animals or one another.

I can see why the cows chose you. It makes a nice myth in itself.

Marion Woodman

Marion Woodman is among a dozen or so Jungian analysts on this continent whose work has burst the confines of the professional community and appealed to a much wider audience. Her three books on eating disorders—*The Owl Was a Baker's Daughter*, *Addiction to Perfection*, and *The Pregnant Virgin*—have helped guide thousands of women back from the brink of self-destruction and into a more fulfilling relationship with their own femininity. For it is precisely the repression of the feminine, Woodman believes, that has cut us off from nature and the wisdom of our bodies.

Woodman's interest in eating disorders, and in addictions in general, stems from painful personal experience. After struggling with anorexia as a young woman, she suffered a near physical breakdown in middle age that forced her to give up her career as a high school English teacher and travel to Europe to seek a cure. After a year of Jungian analysis in England, she went to Zurich, Switzerland, where her own dreams guided her on the path to self-healing. "They told me to take the positive metaphors they offered and allow their energy to work in my body," she says, comparing this approach to Carl Simonton's, whose method for helping cancer patients heal themselves was largely unknown at the time.

While in Zurich, Woodman decided to complete training as a Jungian analyst and return to Canada to practice. Since her return in 1979, she has specialized in the treatment of addictions of all kinds, and her work with clients has convinced her that the addict's real search is not for a particular substance, but for meaning in life, and food for the hungry soul. "Soul lives on metaphor," Woodman explains. She is a frequent (and extremely popular) presenter at conferences throughout North America.

Our interview takes place across the dining room table of a friend in West Los Angeles, where Woodman has stopped briefly on her way elsewhere. She is a mature woman, poised yet quite accessible, and she speaks with fervor of the deep suffering that leads to, and stems from, addiction.

Outside, a thunderstorm (a freak occurrence in these parts) shatters the suburban calm as we talk and sets a neighbor dog to howling. As we raise our voices over the din, we marvel at the rich soul metaphors the environment itself can sometimes provide.

Marion Woodman

Addiction to Perfection

What does it mean to be addicted?

Addicted individuals are being driven by an inner energy toward a particular object—be it alcohol, food, drugs, money, or another person. This object is a substitute for something that remains unknown to them; the object is actually the presence of something absent—the presence of an absence. So the more they have, the more they need; the more filled up they become, the emptier they feel.

How do you account for this haunting sense of absence?

In both the East and the West, there is a deeply rooted desire or need to transcend who we are. Some higher power, some God, finds us unacceptable as we are. We've spent several thousand years learning the arts of self-transcendence. Built into that self-transcendence is a search for the Absolute. We feel ourselves morally obliged to search for this and to make our lives answerable to it. Heroes in fairytales, Arthur's Knights of the Round Table, and now space heroes search for it. "May the Force be with you" is their benediction as they lift off to never-never land.

Addictions are based on a longing for presence. Addicts somehow believe they can live in the presence of perfection—the perfect body, the perfect man or woman, the perfect nirvana. Addictions aren't just an escape from something intolerable. They're archetypally based on the search for perfection, for the Sun God, for the Holy Grail. Most people believe that any person worth his or her salt will go on this search.

Are there certain disciplines associated with this search?

Yes. Hatha yoga can be one, especially when it's misunderstood, as it often is in the West. We Westerners tend to forget that people in the East are generally much more rooted lin their bodies, and their spiritual disciplines *assume* that rootedness. People who are already in their heads can misuse yoga to take them even farther out of their bodies. I do yogas asanas myself and encourage my analysands to do them, but only with a competent teacher who recognizes the danger of misusing these disciplines to reach a disembodied bliss consciousness free of our limitations. Our limitations are crucial to who we are. They are our friends, not our enemies.

Say a little more about the danger involved.

I'm all for being in harmony with all things, but too often the conditions for that harmony aren't present, and the individual doesn't have the discipline to create the conditions. For example, the junkie on a high may experience himself to be in harmony with all things, but in fact he has no clear perception of the things he claims to be in harmony with. He's merely fantasizing. Likewise, yoga practitioners can go into a fantasy, using yoga to escape reality and leave their bodies behind.

How does this relate to other addictions?

Addictive behavior begins with a yearning to belong—to be a real person in a real situation. But in our society, perfection is confused with reality. Unless you pretend to be perfect, you don't belong; you're considered weird, neurotic, unfit. In the dysfunctional family that pretends to be happy, where food is the center of the family gathering, one child may become a binger, another an anorexic, another a bulimic. The harmony and perfection that everyone pretends is present at the meal is in fact absent, but everyone denies the absence, and the young child, doubting his or her own perceptions, seeks the harmony through food. Denial is fundamental in addictive families: denial of what is not present, the loving family; and denial of what is present, the addiction.

Addicted persons have experienced real trauma. They can't trust reality. The ground of reality—their ability to rely on their own perception of what is real—has been pulled out from under them, and there's a legitimate absence of trust at the core of their being. So they're constantly struggling to approximate or simulate reality, and they can't trust their own simulation either, because it keeps changing. What is ultimately real for them is an absence—an absence of reality. The best they can do is simulate its presence.

In the movie *River's Edge*, Dennis Hopper has a companion, Ella, who is a doll. Hopper knows Ella is a doll, and he turns to her and says, "We know that, don't we, Ella?" In his imagination, her gaping mouth answers, "Yes." The audience can see that Ella is a doll, that one of Hopper's legs is plastic, that the relationship is a plastic parody. Whether they can feel in their bones the tragic commentary on our own society depends on how plastic they themselves are. Many people dream that they have plastic limbs, or plastic hearts, or that they are dolls or are in love with dolls. They live in simulated bodies in a simulated world. Nothing ultimately exists except what they've invented, and they have to go on inventing because the absence would be overwhelming. The invention, the simulation, is fulfilling real needs; the doll is a substitute for a real companion. But to get rid of the doll means there is no companion at all. How many love affairs do you know that are pure simulation? Still, they're existence itself to the lovers, because the lovers are so needy.

One question that haunts the addict is, Does anything really exist, apart from my invention of it? In order to get close to the answer, addicts play Russian roulette with themselves. If I put a bullet into a gun and hold it to my head, I have one chance in six of blowing my brains out. If I die, then my question has been answered—something is real, apart from my invention. If I don't, at least I'm living on the edge. This is the game anorexics, gamblers, alcoholics, fast drivers, are playing. It's also the game our culture, our planet, is playing. How close can we come to the edge without going over?

In the movie *The Deer Hunter*, for example, the thesis was that America was on a high, like an addict, and the Vietnam War was this country's Russian roulette. Americans died, and we discovered that yes, there is a reality out there, the world is not just an American invention. There is grace in that; fantasy dies.

And new life begins.

Yes. Looked at from this point of view, the war was one of the most moving things that happened in the history of America. The soldiers came home maimed. Nobody wanted to see them. The conquering hero image was no more. Then the soldiers who had been through the horror, stoned or not, said, "You have to recognize us; we are your life." In the failure of the conquering hero myth is the possibility of new life for the planet. Recognizing our own failure as conquering heroes, we recognize our own humanness. This is true of the street people, too, the bag ladies, the waifs, the outcasts. In dreams, these are the unknowns who carry the new energy. They don't have the power to say, "Be" and it is. They are a part of us, and they are forcing us to realize, culturally and individually, that we must forgo our addiction to omnipotence. To play God is to reject our human reality.

When they finally decided to build a monument in Washington, they had to face this. They couldn't erect statues of soldiers throwing grenades at natives or of soldiers raising the American flag. Such hero imagery is no longer possible; veterans no longer relate to it. Instead, a woman designed a black wall that goes deep into Mother Earth, and on that wall is inscribed every name of every casualty. Finally America has its Wailing Wall. People come to the wall and feel the names of their loved ones with their fingers, their bodies, and they weep. That's what war is about—tears. And that's what life is about—suffering, loss, conflict, joy. The dark and the light. What Keats called the "vale of soul-making."

As long as addicts are trying to transcend themselves, reaching for the sky, pulling away from Earth into spirit, they're like some hero carved in stone, standing on top of his pillar alone, blind to the pigeon shit. Instead of transcending ourselves, we need to move *into* ourselves. We're talking about human unsuccess—not failure, but the unsuccess that is human, in contrast to the perfection that rapes the soul.

I'm aware that the word "soul" has a lot of currency these days, especially in Jungian circles. What does it mean, exactly?

"Soul," to me, means "embodied essence," from the the Latin verb *esse*, to be. It's part spirit and part matter. Blake says that "body is that portion of soul perceived by the five senses." Through the orifices of our bodies, our souls interact with the outer world. Certainly homemade bread and strawberry jam can feed our soul, and so can Mozart. Soul, I think, has to do with the point where time and the timeless intersect, moments when we experience ourselves and others in our full humanity—part animal, part divine. Traditionally, soul is thought of as feminine, as matter is thought of as feminine. So long as we are on this Earth, body and soul are inextricably bound together. Neither is perfect by absolute standards. When that perfectionist ideal starts calling out the orders and laying down the judgments, some delicate feminine creature is raped in our dreams.

Why do you think addiction is so prevalent in our times?

Technology is driving us faster and faster, and it more and more obliterates the individual soul. Centuries of patriarchy and patriarchal values have put the emphasis on goals, achievement, competition, product. Now, of course, we're starting to reject those values, because we're finding that life isn't worth living if we're always running as fast as we can. My therapy practice is made up of people who have finally said, "If this is life, I don't want to live."

Yes, but achievement and productivity are the ideal in our culture. The addict is just an intensified example of a way of being that most of us, in one way or another, have adopted.

Yes. And it has been passed down to us by our parents and our grandparents. Our parents had standards for us, they expected a certain performance, and we tried to live up to their expectations. But when this happens, children learn to perform rather that to be who they are, and the soul goes into hiding—in a manure pile in dreams, for example. As adults, they never think about their own reactions. Instead they wonder, "Who should I please here in order to make the best performance?" After you've pleased mother and father and teacher and husband and boss, you finally get to the point where you start asking, "Who am I?" and "What are my needs?" This is the point where many people recognize that they are on a suicidal journey. Their perfectionist ideals have lured them away from their own life. The underlying question becomes, "Do I want to live?" Some addicts decide that if this is what the world is, they don't want any part of it. Others say, "Yes, I'd like to live, but I have no idea what that means." They are so out of touch with the life force, the sheer joy of being alive. I think most people rarely experience this joy, and, as a result, they are living by will-power. Eventually will-power breaks down, and it's a good thing it does, because then there's a chance for self-cure.

You see, I look at neurosis creatively, as Jung did. A neurosis or an addiction will not allow a person to go on living an empty non-life. Unless the person chooses to be blindly unconscious, eventually he or she asks, "What is this compulsion that is destroying me?" and, even more important, "Who am I?"

So there's a wisdom in the addiction, ultimately.

Yes, if the person takes the time to find it. I really like working with addicts, because they're desperate, and they have fierce energy. Their dreams are full of wolves, and mythologically the wolf is the animal of Apollo, the sun god and also the god of creativity. These wolves represent a ferocious hunger for something; the addict doesn't know what it is. From a Jungian perspective, the psyche naturally moves toward wholeness. If we become stuck in a way of life that is not right for us, or a psychological attitude that we've outgrown, then symptoms appear that force us out of our nest, if we're willing to deal with them. If we choose not to, then we become obsessed with something that concretizes a genuine spiritual need.

Jung, for example, worked with one of the founders of AA. "The craving for alcohol," he wrote, "[is] the equivalent, on a low level, of the spiritual thirst of our being for wholeness; expressed in medieval language: the union with God." Alcohol, he pointed out, is *spiritus* in Latin. If that wolf energy can be lovingly disciplined and turned in the right direction, it can be powerfully healing and creative. That's what the addict's journey is all about—it's a spiritual search that's become perverted. You see it in the rituals that addicts engage in. If you work with these rituals creatively, you will often find profound religious activity going on there.

Give an example of a ritual that an addict might perform.

Well, real bingers will not tell anybody what they're going to do on Friday night, but they will plan very carefully the food they're going to eat. Usually it includes something sweet, something made with milk, and something made with grain. These are exactly the foods used in the ancient goddess rituals. Often they'll wear a particular ritual outfit; they'll disconnect the telephone, lock themselves in their room, and begin eating, consciously at first. But at the point where instinct can no longer be disciplined, they lose consciousness and start wolfing food down. They don't taste it; they don't want it; they want oblivion. But, you see, there's tremendous excitement before the binge begins, tremendous anticipation that they're about to move out of the unbearable two-dimensional world and into the presence of divine sweetness and nourishment. Metaphorically, this is the divine Mother. In sacred ritual, the ego crosses into sacred space and surrenders to the divine. That's the whole point. When the god enters, the ego opens and expands, and although it returns to profane space when the ritual is over, it has touched into a timeless world that gives depth and meaning to this one.

Addicts' rituals focus on a concrete god—alcohol, gambling, hedonism—that annihilates their ego and drives them into meaningless unconsciousness. When they wake up, they feel duped. Instead of being connected to a richer meaning in their life, they are further alienated and alone. Their self-esteem plummets, and they drop into the suicidal fantasies so characteristic of addicts. Their basic impulse is a natural one— to find another dimension—but they have the wrong god. For most people the Judeo-Christian tradition no longer holds the numinosity, the light, the consciousness that enriches the soul. So they're trying to find it in their own living room.

You talk in several of your books about the relationship to the mother and about mothering that fails to contain and hold the infant in a loving way. How does that contribute to addiction?

Enormously. A mother who doesn't love her own body is not connected to her own life energy. She cannot mirror her child in its own beingness, and therefore cannot connect the child to its own feelings in its own body. The child doesn't develop a strong container with firm boundaries. Ultimately it's cut off from its own inner life. Mother is *mater*, and few of us love our own matter.

And this love of our own matter is transmitted from the mother?

Yes. But very few mothers have it in our culture, because they didn't receive it from their mothers. And that's not to lay a guilt trip on mothers. Many women feel tremendous guilt about their mothering, but they can't give what they weren't given. Look at the treatment of the feminine principle in our culture: People say they care, yet they rape Mother Earth at such a pace that we could end up destroying ourselves in our blind stupidity.

In that sense, the entire socioeconomic system is involved in a kind of addiction. We're destroying ourselves in a binge of consumption.

Yes. Mired in matter, concretized *mater* (mother), which compensates for the patriarchal demand for perfection. The more we try to transcend ourselves, the more we are unconsciously trapped in our own materialism. Microcosm and macrocosm mirror each other. Just as we rape our own bodies, we rape our Earth. We put cement over her, we destroy her rain forests, her ozone layer. Meanwhile both men and women dream incessantly of being raped. What does that mean metaphorically? It means that our feminine body/soul is being ravaged by a power principle that doesn't care one bit what happens to us as human beings. The feminine soul that would move with the majestic rhythms of nature into creative, whole living is considered slow, stupid, and irrational.

In some way, then, mothers have to affirm a love of life in order to transmit this love to their children.

But they can't if they have no idea there's anything to life but performance. One of my clients told me a story about how he came home from school very late once as a small boy because he had stopped by the river and found some beautiful little stones. He had filled his pockets with them and come running home to give them to his mother. She was furious with him and turned him upside down and shook him, and the stones went all over. "Now pick them up," she told him, "and throw them out in the lane where they belong." Well, that was traumatic for him, because he truly loved those stones. They had a numinosity for him, and his mother had no sense at all that he was offering his soul to her. She rejected his beingness. No mother would do that purposely, I would hope. But if she doesn't have that inner sense herself, she can't support it in her child.

So there's no one to blame. It's just that this is what has been transmitted from generation to generation.

It's the world we're living in. And it's our responsibility to become conscious and stop it. The feminine is rumbling with rage and grief. The frenzied addict eventually has to look her in the eye. And so does our frenzied world. We have to discover the magnificent consciousness in matter, and in our own bodies. We are capable of seeing the light in a rose bush, of feeling the energy in a tree. We are born to live in the love that permeates all life.

What is the alternative for your analysands who have addictive problems? How can they heal themselves from this negative addictive spiral?

It's a long, hard struggle, because the reality that we are raised in is the only reality we know. We act toward ourselves and others as we were acted upon. If the authority figures in our childhood acted out of power, demanding the best little boy or girl, the best little scholar, the best little athlete, the child introjects that power and constantly criticizes, evaluates, and judges himself or herself. An inner voice is constantly saying, "Who I am is not lovable. I must do something special in order to deserve love. I'm not good enough, I should be better, I should be able to make a faster decision, I should have more courage, I should, I ought to, I have to." A person can learn to recognize that voice and separate it from his or her essence, can learn to say, "That's not me saying that, it's my unconscious parent blathering inside my head. I can concentrate on hearing my own voice, my own needs, my own feelings." That's when healing begins.

First of all, though, it seems you'd need enough perspective to be able to see the part that's tormenting you, as well as a willingness or desire to disidentify from it. Otherwise there must be a very strong tendency to get sucked right back into it, to say, "Okay, you're right, I totally agree with you, I'm a worthless piece of shit."

Exactly. That's the old pattern, and I don't know any way out of it if you don't have a creative outlet. You have to find your own way of expressing who you are.

You can't face that compulsive part of you head on?

You can, but you'll lose. It's an evil energy that wants to rob us of our life. Facing it directly constellates its negative power.

So we need to use soul-making to strengthen our own soul, and let that be a kind of shield or protection against the evil.

If you promise to limit yourself to 500 calories a day, or to quit smoking or drinking, all you do is strengthen the unconscious, which says, "No, I'm not going to do what you say." You set up a series of polarities that can't possibly be resolved—everything is either all black or all white, you're either completely sober or you're out of control—and you're swung back and forth between these two poles. It's a very patriarchal way of seeing things.

It's literally a "set-up," because pretty soon the unconscious will overcome the ego, and your will-power will be destroyed.

Yes, and if you've lived with an addiction all your life, you have a very weak ego to begin with. As I see it, the feminine way is the healing way. Rather than polarizing, the feminine accepts the paradox: This is beautiful; *that* is the opposite, and that too is beautiful. Our culture says that thin is beautiful, but that doesn't mean that fat people are ugly. In fact, many people are diminished when they lose weight. Every body has its right size for the amount of energy it contains. The problem is to keep the energy flowing instead of blocking it in fat.

In some way, then, the body has a wisdom such that if left to itself it will choose its natural size.

And the body also has a wisdom such that it recognizes when the soul is so frightened, and so unable to cope with the world, that it has to have some kind of soporific. The food or the alcohol or the drugs are keeping the pain down or keeping the fear away. Or excess body weight may act as armor to protect the soul. Women, for example, who quickly lose a hundred pounds may suddenly find themselves attractive to men. If they haven't developed psychically, they are like five-year-olds in a mature body. The child can't deal with the sexuality, so the body takes on weight again for protection. Or it breaks out in a rash, or vaginitis, or some other symptom. The truth is, the body is the best friend we have, although most of us think it's our worst enemy. It's like a donkey that gets beaten again and again, but it still tries to hold whatever balance it can.

When you talk about trying to subdue the addiction through will power, I think of the first of the Twelve Steps of AA, which says that we admitted we were powerless over our life, and that through will-power alone we couldn't do anything about it.

Right. There's the addict, who wants control above all else, having to admit to his powerlessness. But it's the first step.

I have immense respect for AA. Many of the addicts I'm working with are in Alcoholics Anonymous or Overeaters Anonymous. And the Twelve Steps are the natural progression that emerges in dreams. Where I think my work complements AA is in its emphasis on creativity and the feminine mode—the soul-making we talked of earlier. You sit down and listen to your own body. You reflect on your day, you write, you paint, you put your soul down on paper or into your music or your dancing or your sculpting, whatever your creative outlets may be. You become so interested in nourishing and releasing the inner being that you're not driven to the refrigerator or the liquor cabinet. Or course, it can take immense discipline to say, "Stop it."

What about the importance of imagination in the soul-making process?

Soul work is an act of the imagination. The soul lives on metaphor. For example, you've seen great athletes stand still and imagine themselves doing a dive or clearing the high bar, then go into the actual dive or jump. If they can't see themselves completing it, they know they won't be able to. Addicts suffer from failure of the imagination. They become imprisoned in rigid attitudes. They can't imagine freedom. Because they deny reality, they can't change it. They fail to make the necessary rites of passage from one stage of life to another, fail to mature, fail to get out of boring jobs or destructive relationships. They fail to see the meaning of what they are living. Their dreams would tell them, if they would pay attention. The metaphors in dreams give us a picture of our psychic condition and how to change it.

So through metaphor the body talks to the spirit and the spirit talks to the body. I notice you use the word "metaphor" and not "symbol."

They are basically the same thing. I like the word "metaphor" because it comes from the Greek for "transformer." And that's exactly what a metaphor is: It transforms one kind of energy into another. Soul work is incarnation, the process of spirit incarnating in the body. The spirit is in the body for however long we live and has its work to do while we are here. But many people just obliterate soul. They drive as fast as they can at their work or whatever their particular addictive behavior may be, and the soul becomes more and more frenzied. As the soul becomes more frenzied, the body becomes more frenzied, because the soul lives in the body.

So we are filling up our lives with material things, with doing and accomplishing, and not heeding the soul's need of metaphor—for aesthetic experience, poetry, being in nature, silence, writing, and so forth.

Yes. Anything creative. If you give yourself half an hour a day with your dreams or your music—whatever your creative process—the soul becomes very quiet. You're located in your body and you feel nourished by the activity. Addiction, in contrast, thrives on frenzy. The faster the person goes, the greater the frenzy, whereas to become quiet and live with these metaphors is to go back to your own creating.

Much of my work with addicts centers on trying to find the metaphor that the addictive object represents for them and then encouraging them to bring that metaphor to consciousness. Alcohol, for example, represents the spirit that the addict longs for. Food, I think, is very often the positive mother, the positive mother the addict didn't have.

The same with compulsive relationships, where there is a longing for wholeness through union with another person—the other person carries the projection of that totality in concrete form. In working with metaphor, I try to take a powerful image from the dream and have the person concentrate on it, meditate on it, perceive it, reflect on it. Meditation on the metaphor objectifies the energy and thus transforms it. Particularly with psychosomatic problems, metaphor is often a very powerful healer. By imagining the metaphor in the body and concentrating on it, new energy is released. Matter and spirit cooperate in the healing process.

An anorexic, for example, may dream that there's going to be a wedding, but the wedding can't take place until some work is done. She doesn't know what the work is, but until it's done, the spiritual eye must remain veiled, the forehead shielded. Then she's told she has to go down and clean up the garbage in the basement. Sometimes there's a cat lost in the furnace pipes, or a little girl buried underneath a pile of manure, and she's starving, she has huge eyes, and she looks into the dreamer's eyes and says, "You're trying to kill me." In other words, before the dreamer can continue on her spiritual search, she has to clean up the garbage in her basement, at the deepest levels in her body, the deepest levels of soul. She has to come to terms with the starving child inside.

Very often there's a huge snake down there as well, which represents kundalini, and the dreamer is awestruck by this incredible serpent power. A connection has to be made at the deepest body level before the inner marriage can take place. It is dangerous if we try to fly into spirit before we're grounded in the body. Too much light too fast, and we're blown away. That's what happens to genuine anorexics. They hate their filthy bodies. They want so much spirit, so much light, that they'll starve themselves into euphoria and then run and hyperventilate in order to get it. But they're being carried off the Earth, and they've vacated the body entirely.

And that's why creativity can be so healing. Because in order to be creative, in order to engage in soul-making, you have to listen to your body.

Exactly. True creativity, true soul-making, comes from that deep communication with what Jung would call the archetypal world. That's where the real nourishment is. But to be in the body also means to suffer, and that's why most addicts are trying to avoid it.

Say a little more about that.

Well, I think the word "love" is just bandied around in our culture. To me, real love, the move from power to love, involves immense suffering. Any creative work comes from that level, where we share our suffering, just the sheer suffering of being human. And that's where the real love is.

Compassion, of course, means "to suffer with."

Yes. But not at a superficial level. Addicts are so busy trying to find something on the surface that they never take the time to drop into process where the real healing happens. They never stop long enough to allow presence, to be in the present. They live either in a fantasized paradise that is past or in a fantasized glorious future. They lock themselves into one rigid way of behaving in an attempt to get control of their lives, all the time terrified that they'll lose control, and denying the fact that they already have. "If only I could lose weight, if only he loved me, if only I could stop drinking, if only . . ." is the cry that silently breaks their heart. Real imagination is at work when one day the addict can say, "I am. I am loved. I can receive love. I do love myself. I do love."

I remember when that realization struck me. It was as if Niagara Falls had broken open my heart, and I was a frail atom in the universe with some incredible energy pounding through me. That night I dreamed of a tidal wave relentlessly pushing its way. On its crest was an immense chocolate-colored woman, her magnificent arm upraised like Delacroix's "Liberty." She was moving in and nothing could stop her. Then I was a molecule in the wave, in harmony with countless other molecules. We were all empowered with the love that would bring her to land.

That's where I think the healing is. We're being forced out of our tiny individual, cultural, and national boxes, and we're beginning to dream of an embodied consciousness, a global harmony that resonates through everything. That's the real bridge between disembodied spirit and unconscious matter.

Could you elaborate?

Well, as I see it, we're all addicts, because we experience ourselves as emptiness swinging in empty space between spirit and matter. Located nowhere. Someone, something out there must have the answer. The more our spirit attempts to escape from this impossible world by transcendence or theorizing (fantasizing or fanaticism), the more our animal body compensates by becoming a garbage disposal, consuming everything we stuff into it. We're the children of a creator, yes, but we're also the children of a creatrix. Until we know her through the metaphors born of our own sacred matter, we're trapped in our own void. The healing power lies in the metaphor. The creative imagination binds together the physical and spiritual, all that is spirit being pictured in the flesh. When Matisse was asked whether he believed in God, his response was, "Yes, when I'm painting."

Sam Keen

Sam Keen is a writer, philosopher, lecturer, professional gadfly, and theologian who, in a dozen books over the last 25 years, has brought his unique blend of psychological acumen, cultural observation, and an existential bent for asking penetrating questions to studies of spirituality, war, love, hate—and, most recently, men.

In his earlier work—filled, as are most of his writings, with personal anecdotes and reflections—Keen investigates the nature of the religious experience, the origins of our sense of wonder and mystery. Later, in *The Passionate Life*, he maps out what he calls "the stages of loving" and the ways we mature into love. In *Faces of the Enemy*, his next book, he explores the "hostile imagination" that drives us to war, showing that "love is infinitely creative but hate is not inventive at all." The book was made into a documentary that was aired over PBS.

Just as he took up the topic of hate after completing a book on love, Keen segued from enemies to men when he began examining the rhetoric of war and peace. "The ideological brand of feminism was making war a gender issue, a male problem, something men engage in," he says. "Women were naturally gentle, networking, and nurturing, in this view, and men were nasty, brutish, and innately hostile. If we would just leave the world to women, we wouldn't have war."

"Isn't that true?" I tease.

"Not for the women I know," he shoots back. "The tradeoffs in gender in our society are tradeoffs everybody conspires to create and sustain. Ever since the beginning of recorded history, men have been socialized to be warriors."

In his latest book, *Fire in the Belly,* Keen endeavors to separate the warrior ethic and the forces that compel us to wage war from the innate characteristics of men. In the process, he issues a challenge, both to the women's movement and to the incipient men's movement, to reconsider cherished assumptions about what it means to be a man. We're all in this together, he suggests. Rather than blaming one another for our problems, we need to join in envisioning a new order in which human beings are a peaceful and sustainable presence on Earth.

Keen's early life, he recalls, was shaped by two major influences: being a perpetual outsider in a succession of small Southern towns and playing in the woods among wild things. It was in the woods that he gained his earliest sense of the sacred and of the deep connection between the sacred and the natural world.

Brought up in a fundamentalist but "well-read" Presbyterian family where "one was expected to think the right things but to have thought them through," Keen studied at Harvard Divinity School with the great Protestant theologian Paul Tillich and then earned a doctorate in philosophy at Princeton. After teaching philosophy and the philosophy of religion for a number of years, he moved to California (his "spiritual home") in the late '60s, where he came under the thrall of Esalen and the human potential movement. Some difficult years of self-searching followed, and he eventually left academia to become a "freelance philosopher" and a contributing editor of *Psychology Today* in its heyday, interviewing such luminaries as Arica founder Oscar Ichazo and Tibetan Buddhist master Chogyam Trungpa.

Handsome, robust, graying, Keen speaks with a resonant voice and an air of authority that recall his theological training; and his outspoken criticisms of political and religious establishments, both Eastern and Western, reflect the Protestant prophetic tradition in which he was raised. A rancher by avocation, a lover of horses, and a man of the earth—he loves to point out that "human" is related to the Latin word "humus," meaning "earth"—Keen is also a sometime practitioner of hatha yoga and his "own crazy brand of t'ai chi," whose favorite meditation is taking long walks in the woods.

The following is a composite of two interviews conducted on two separate occasions nearly five years apart. The first took place in the offices of Fantasy Records in Berkeley, California, where Keen was videotaping

Faces of the Enemy for PBS. The second occurred on a quiet autumn afternoon in the hills of Sonoma, California, on the ranch Keen shares with his wife, Jananne Lovett, their daughter, Jessamyn, and assorted horses, dogs, and other animals.

Sam Keen

The Passionate Life

In The Passionate Life *you argue that passion is an important aspect not just of sexuality but of all our affairs, all our life situations. I was wondering how you see the relationship between passion and the spiritual life.*

When we think of passion in this culture, we normally think of its sexual connotations—or occasionally of a passionate singer or a passionate actor. I use the term "passionate life" as a synonym for the spirited life, which is the opposite of the disspirited life, the opposite of a life of boredom and self-absorption, a life that is totally measured and controlled by the self. The passionate life involves surrendering, being taken over by something larger than ourselves; it involves losing ourselves, which is at the same time also finding ourselves.

A passionate life, however, is not necessarily a good thing. I would rather have a mediocre moderation than the wrong kind of passion. Fundamentalists are very passionate, but their passion borders on fanaticism. Plato makes the distinction between heavenly eros and demonic eros. The wrong kind of passion, the wrong kind of love, can destroy life, just as the right kind of love can be fulfilling. We continually have to ask ourselves, "Is this love—this person or movement or thing to which I am surrendering and opening myself—demonic or divine, fulfilling or destructive?"

In the spirited life, we're trying to become permeable to the world around us, trying, in Buddhist terms, to allow ourselves to be moved by all sentient beings. But if we devote ourselves exclusively to a single cause or a single person—what Plato called demonic eros—we create disharmony between ourselves and our world—and that can be terribly destructive.

There's an old story about a cowboy who is asked how to ride a horse. "You know," he says, "it's real easy. It's just like dancing with a girl, except you let the horse lead." In that sense, authentic passion is like dancing with the world, the inspirited world, but letting the world lead. In Chinese terms, we're trying to discover the Tao to which we should conform our lives.

What about passion in intimate relationships? Is this compatible with spiritual practice?

Many spiritual traditions say that you shouldn't be intimate with another person, certainly not sexually intimate, because that would prevent you from devoting yourself exclusively to God. In a sense, they're afraid that the attachment would become demonic—which is an inevitable temptation when relationships are sexual.

But I believe that the essence of the life of the spirit is the life of relationship. The opposite, the disspirited life, is one in which we become encapsulated within the self, caught up in the character armor, identified with the personality. The life of the spirit is one in which we realize that to be is to be in relationship. The question is not whether we have intimate relationships, but whether those relationships are creative or destructive.

In fact, the two millstones that grind down the ego best are a committed love relationship and a child. The moment you commit yourself to a relationship, lots of things happen that don't happen when you're casual. In our world we don't normally say to another person, "I accept you for better or worse, richer or poorer, in sickness and in health." Normally all our love is conditional: "I'll accept you as long as you provide for me, as long as you don't put on five pounds, as long as you dye your hair red, as long as you believe the same things I believe." But when I say, "I accept you for better or for worse," the part of me that all my life has been hiding the worst, has been on my best behavior for fear of being disliked or rejected, starts bringing out some of the worst. Where I'd been so nice and attentive before, now I become controlling or critical or demanding. Instead of two romantic lovers, we now have two romantics who are dealing with some of the ugliest, most infantile parts of themselves.

What's the virtue of that?

The virtue of that is that marriage is designed to let two people fall out of love and into reality. The virtue of that is that what has been hidden is now revealed. You said you wanted to get rid of your ego, your pretenses, your mask, your performance. Well, all right, here's your opportunity. Because when you're living with someone 24 hours a day, you can't maintain the facade.

So a committed relationship really confronts you with what Jung calls the shadow, the dark and unacknowledged parts of the psyche.

Yes, it confronts you with your shadow in an unavoidable way. Of course, you can get a divorce, you can run away, but then the shadow just goes deeper. The French philosopher Gustave Thibon says, "Vanity runs, love digs. If you fly away from yourself, your prison will run with you and will close in because of the wind of your flight; if you go deep down into yourself, it will disappear in paradise." When you make a commitment—to a marriage or a home or a farm or an occupation or a vocation—you have an opportunity to "go deep down" and find out what you're really like.

Ultimately, marriage or intimacy is exactly like the spirited life because it isn't about understanding each other, it isn't about knowing. To the contrary, the more I am committed to someone, the less, in a sense, I know them. As I come to accept them more and more, I come to realize that there are places in them that I will never know.

I used to think that men and women were essentially alike, and that if we just got rid of the conditioning and gave dolls to boys and hammers to girls and didn't use sexist language . . . but I don't think that anymore. More and more I've come to believe that we are deep and abiding mysteries to each other.

The German poet Rainer Maria Rilke says that one of the great gifts that two people can give to one another is to stand guard over one another's solitude.

Yes, that's the other side. Real intimacy is always in dialogue with solitude.

How does the rhythm of intimacy and solitude, merging and then distancing or separating, fit into a close, committed relationship?

You can only merge with someone if you can also separate. The more you can enter into deep solitude, the more fully you can merge with another person.

I noticed in the early years of my most meaningful relationships that when we would make love and it was particularly good and melting and merging, we would frequently fight afterward. In those days I didn't have a private place of my own. In the last few years I've had a separate studio—and I also travel. The physical being away, the spaces between us, are as important as the coming together. We can't possible satisfy all of each other's needs. We're so plural.

If you've lost your solitude, you've lost that place of silence and of waiting, of thinking and of weighing and measuring your own experience, and of determining whether you're on or off path.

What about balancing one's personal, individual path with the demands of a committed relationship? Sometimes one's path calls on one to act in certain ways; on the other hand, a committed relationship has a certain form, it needs to be nurtured and maintained.

That's where negotiation comes in. Any couple has to negotiate their own conditions—and those conditions are very different for different people. For example, there are long-distance lovers and short-distance lovers. What distance do you need in order to maintain intimacy? I knew one woman who was married to a ship's captain, and they had a marvelous marriage. But they could only see each other six or seven weeks a year. I know other people who don't ever want to spend a night apart. My own rhythm is that I need a certain number of nights apart—to catch my dreams, for example.

Another lovely thing about intimate relationships is that the body is involved, and the body has its own wisdom, its own ways of melting the ego. Loving sexuality is a real elixir, a real dissolver of ego, especially after the initial stages of intensity. In the beginning sex is exciting. Then, after a while, sex becomes normal. A lot of people have a crisis at this point, because they have been so conditioned to expect intensity in sexuality that when intensity goes, they think there's something wrong with the relationship. But there isn't—it's just that sexuality comes to reflect, on an almost one-to-one basis, the character of the relationship. In the beginning we can fool ourselves. Sex can be more intense and interesting than we are.

Sex, then, becomes a kind of barometer or indicator of the quality and the intensity of the connection between two people, and of their connection with the world around them.

Exactly.

What about the dance between the sexes? Particularly right now, after the feminist movement has made inroads into how women feel about themselves, the dynamic between men and women has changed a great deal. Relationships are becoming harder and harder for people to sustain and to find meaning and value in, because the old models no longer apply. What do you see as the challenge for men and women right now?

I don't know that the way in which relationships between men and women have changed has much to do with feminism or the sexual revolution. I think they've changed much more because women have finally bought the message we've been giving them for almost three centuries—that what's valuable is making and manufacturing and succeeding in the marketplace, and that the home and nurturance are of secondary importance. Since the 1970s, the majority of women in the United States have been in the workplace. They've accepted a masculine view of the world and of what has value and meaning. I'm not saying that women should stay home—only that we've devalued the home and nurturance, no matter who does the nurturing. That's had a greater influence than anything else.

As we have devalued nurturing and created a society based primarily upon competition and not upon care, we have placed an enormous burden on intimacy. Someone once said that sex is the only green thing left in a world of concrete. Because it is so care-less out there, we seek all of our caring from a single intimate relationship. But no one relationship can possible satisfy all our needs for caring and intimacy.

Perhaps it's because we can't be intimate with ourselves, can't be intimate with the natural world, can't be intimate with our co-workers, that we place such a burden on intimate relationships.

Yes. What we've lost in modern society is a sense of living in the center of a world to which we feel intimately connected.

In Fire in the Belly, *you argue that men are not innately predisposed to be warriors. But what about our biological makeup, our musculature, our genital anatomy, our testosterone levels? Do you really believe there's a natural distribution of warriorlike tendencies among men and women?*

In the first place, I think we make an enormous mistake by failing to distinguish between hostility and aggression. Certainly people are naturally aggressive, which simply means that we naturally focus our energy toward the achievement of certain goals. Writing a book is just as aggressive as hitting somebody, but it's not hostile. In that sense it may be true that males have more aggression, more focused energy. And because we have a larger muscle mass, our ways of storing and discharging energy are different from women's. Clearly their bodies are softer and more rounded than ours, and their brain structure is more bilateral, which means their right and left hemispheres are in greater communication. Ejaculation is a good metaphor for the way male bodies store and then purge energy, whereas a woman's pattern of energy usage is more rhythmic, more akin to the pattern found in primitive societies, where the body doesn't hold tension as much, but discharges it more evenly.

But I don't think this difference is necessarily innate. When men have what Wilhelm Reich called their "character armor" reduced through bodywork techniques like rolfing, their pattern of energy usage also becomes more rhythmic and rounded. In any case, all you have to do is find one culture in which men are not molded into warriors and are therefore not warlike to falsify the biological hypothesis.

Although you could say that in such a culture they've been acculturated to go against their natural biological tendencies, whereas in other cultures they tend to go with their biological tendencies.

You could, but that's a fallacious argument, like saying that, since men are innately warlike and women are innately peaceful, Margaret Thatcher had to be culturally induced to violate her natural nurturing (female) nature and act in a warlike (male) way.

Which may in fact be the case. In any event, wouldn't you agree that in the majority of cultures men are the aggressors, the more hostile ones?

I think it would be more accurate to say that in the majority of cultures men are socialized to go to war. And then we need to ask, What does it do to the bodies and psyches of men over the millennia to socialize them to be warriors? Obviously, the first thing it does is create character armor. The rites of passage in a warrior society are inevitably brutal; the young male is wounded—cut, scourged, circumcised, beaten—in order to teach him not to feel, to cut himself off from his body.

This happens when a boy is just entering puberty.

Usually. If you're eventually going to expect a man to fight, kill, and die for the tribe, it's necessary to desensitize him. In our culture it begins with statements like "Big boys don't cry" or "Stand up and fight like a man." As a result, the boy learns to tighten the jaw to keep from crying, to hold in the anus, to stiffen the arms in preparation for fighting back, to pull up the chest and harden around the heart to keep from being hurt.

Once you train one gender to specialize in a certain set of emotions, you create a dynamic in which the other gender specializes in the other set. In this artificial division, the male is assigned the hard emotions—to be sharp, clear, rational, to set limits, to define things, to act and take responsibility in the public arena—and the female is assigned the softer emotions—to be nurturing, sensitive, intuitive, compassionate, all those things men aren't. Pretty soon we've started characterizing these qualities as masculine and feminine and we get all that confusing Jungian language. Then, once I've defined tenderness and nurturing as feminine, I as a man have to go looking for my "feminine side."

So you don't think such language is helpful.

Not at all. I don't have a "feminine" side. There's nothing feminine about me, as far as I've been able to discover. When I was in Jungian therapy, I looked long and hard to find my feminine side. Finally I realized I was being brainwashed because everything luscious and endearing was being called feminine. When I pick up my daughter to cuddle her, by what stretch of the imagination is that a feminine act? That's as much a part of my maleness as riding my horse down the side of a mountain at breakneck speed.

What about masculinity and femininity in the broader sense of yin and yang? Many Jungians would say that we're not talking about men and women but about a broader dichotomy in which yin represents the more receptive, nurturing, surrendering, yielding side, and yang represents . . .

I just refuse to put any kind of genderal predicates on these qualities. Sure there's a yin and a yang, but don't confuse them with masculine and feminine. Otherwise you begin to ask all the wrong questions, like "Am I manly enough? Am I overly masculine?" instead of asking "What kind of a person am I? Where do I need to learn softness and yielding, and where do I need to learn more toughness and decisiveness?"

But let me get back to my analysis of how the male has been formed by the warrior ethic. The character armor in our bodies that cuts off feeling also shapes our minds to think linearly, to use either-or logic. I believe this mode of thinking is culturally conditioned, rather than biologically determined, and I hypothesize that men could be trained to have more bilateral brains, like women's, in a generation or two.

Is there evidence to support your hypothesis?

Some. For example, when English-speaking men have a stroke in the area of the brain that controls language, they become aphasic, they can no longer speak. Whereas women with the same kind of stroke don't become aphasic. Interestingly, Navaho and Hopi men, like women, also do not become aphasic. Their language is much more pictorial than ours; it comes out of a different part of the brain and a different view of reality. I don't think we know enough yet to separate what I would call the hard-wiring of men and women from the mythic software.

In *Fire in the Belly* I trace what it means to shape men in this way and then look at the three rites of passage men undergo: warfare, work, and sex. War is the most significant. All men are wounded by the warrior ethic, whether we've been to war or not, because if we weren't fighters we were made to feel that we weren't tough enough and were therefore sissies and failures.

Even when we're not at war, the warrior ethic still seems to prevail in our macho, football-oriented culture.

That's right. And business is just warfare in slow motion. The other day I picked up a book on the newsstand entitled *Waging Business Warfare: How to Become a Master of Strategy in Today's Corporate Killing Fields and Win the War for Success.* We're in a culture where men continue to be rewarded for the same set of hostile, paranoid virtues and where women have until recently been rewarded for lacking or not developing them.

You've talked about war and work. What about the third initiation, sex?

Even sex in our culture tends to be centered around competition and conquest. You remember the locker room talk—how many women, how often, how much. I never once heard a boy in my youth talk about how much pleasure he received in sex, or how much pleasure he gave to a woman.

What about the so-called men's consciousness movement? I know you choose not to identify with it, but I wondered what you thought of it.

There is the beginning of a men's movement, but it hasn't gone very deep yet. For more than 25 years, the women's movement has fostered an enormous outpouring of creativity. Women have rethought language, reinterpreted history, reshaped literary criticism, reexamined politics. They've recreated the world in terms of a woman's perspective, restoring what had been left out. All that men have discovered so far is their grief.

In women, the most repressed emotion was aggression, so it was natural that the women's liberation movement would reclaim the angular emotions like anger. For men, what was repressed was the private world of feeling, especially feelings of sorrow and grief. That's precisely what the warrior is not allowed to feel.

Big boys don't cry.

Right. Unfortunately, the emphasis on recovering grief makes the men's movement seem insubstantial at times, as if we're whining. The grieving has been very therapeutic for many men, but it has gotten somehow strangely mixed with a victim ideology. Notice, for instance, how closely aligned are the men's consciousness and adult children of alcoholics movements.

So the men's movement is in its infancy, and it's natural that men are exploring all the emotions we weren't allowed to feel. The problem is, exploring our feelings doesn't give us any political project, any way of re-creating a strong and virile sense of manhood and a man's vocation in the world. Every age in history has had an objective vocation by which manhood was defined. There was man as hunter, man as planter, man as warrior, rational man (homo sapiens), technological man, each stage calling for some elemental virtue not found in the earlier stages.

Now we're in a new era, and we're faced with a new historical vocation, a new hero's journey, one you can read off the front page of the *New York Times* any day of the week. To have dignity, men must accomplish two major tasks. First, we have to stop the game of war and go beyond the warrior ethic. If I'm wrong, you won't be around to prove it. Because we've been so ingenious in creating new weapons, we've worked our way out of that game.

The second task is closely aligned with the first—we have to become husbands of the Earth once again. Out of our ingenuity, we've created the kind of technology that will destroy our ecosystem if we don't learn how to tame it. What would a man look like if he didn't have a Promethean psyche that was always grasping for more and striving to conquer? We're at the beginning of an entirely new era where the definition of manhood has to change.

Or perhaps that same Promethean quality can be redirected toward the inner life, or toward new ways of taking care of the Earth.

Exactly. The warrior energy of men now has to be used paradoxically to destroy the warrior psyche and the politics of warfare. It will require more courage and aggression than we've ever seen on the battlefield.

What about the role of initiation? You mentioned earlier that in a general sense war, work, and sex are rites of passage for men, and you also talk about the brutality of initiation in traditional cultures. What would a more positive, life-affirming initiation look like in our culture? Certainly, among the things we're lacking are appropriate modes of initiation. In fact, many older men don't feel they have anything they can initiate young males into.

There's an awful lot of historical sentimentality about the idea of initiation. I like to put it this way: In primitive societies men really knew who they were. That's the good news. The bad news is, they were mostly wrong about it. And the worst news of all is, they found out who they were because they had the individuality beaten out of them, and the myth of the tribe impressed upon them, so strongly that they never rebelled against it again.

We have very definite rites of passage in our culture, everything from having a first fight to getting a credit card to joining the army. Unfortunately, they initiate us into values that have largely become destructive. And then there is the fact that, lacking formal rites of passage, most of us as young people created informal initiations by finding older people to teach us things, like a grandfather or an uncle or a family friend.

But again, maybe not the right things.

Not necessarily. But now look. One of the things I argue in my book is that our lostness is our strength. When I was growing up, my family moved every two years or so, and I was always an outsider, a stranger, a loner. That early loneliness was my best initiator. I also argue that in the real heroic journey, the second rite of passage has to be self-administered. The first part of this rite of passage, which takes place somewhere near the halfway point in life, is a lonely and intensely individual journey into ourselves. The second part is exactly the opposite. We've got to come back and bring a boon to society. But first we've got to get the boon. On this journey we don't have any set patterns to follow. This is the mark of the initiatory experience of modern man. We have to wrestle in the darkness with our own anxiety and aloneness, without any predetermined models.

So there's a second initiation. The first is an initiation into the values of our culture, but then we have to be born a second time into a spiritual dimension. This idea of the second birth crops up in both the Christian and Hindu traditions. But you're suggesting that we have to come to this second initiation in our own individual way.

Yes, and I think the same is true for women, who also have to go through a second rite of passage which is self-administered in order to have some deep sense of themselves.

You've talked about the hero. Joe Campbell notwithstanding, I tend to associate the hero with the warrior mode, with the individual who accomplishes something through a great deal of striving and struggle. What is the positive view of the hero?

The traditional hero was larger than life. He was a warrior, an artist; he was unusual, unique. In this next period of human history, we need to define the hero quite differently, because it was exactly the individualistic, life-transcending, Promethean hero who got us into the trouble we're in now. The new hero needs to be defined much more ecologically. He's the one who has the courage to fit in. The courage to be contented. The courage to be a part of. The courage not to swell up and try to be larger than life.

The courage to be vulnerable, perhaps?

No, I don't like that word. There's nothing vulnerable about it.

What's wrong with vulnerability?

I don't want to be vulnerable when I shouldn't be. For example, I want to be clever, sly, strategic. A fox isn't vulnerable. He knows how to hide, how to use disguises. A coyote is the least vulnerable animal—even in mythology, coyote is the trickster. The ecological male is not the soft male; he's the dancer, not the warrior. He moves with, rather than against. He's rhythmic, he's flexible, but he isn't vulnerable. I love the image in the *Tao Te Ching* of the sage who can sit and let the mud in the water clear. That person's not vulnerable. To the contrary, he's so strong, he knows how to be silent.

Maybe we have different understandings of what it means to be vulnerable.

To be sensitive, yes, or to be compassionate or responsive.

That's what I think the word vulnerable means.

I prefer responsiveness to vulnerability. The literal meaning of vulnerable is "capable of being wounded; open to attack." God didn't make turtles to take off their shells. For instance, in intimate male-female relationships, men don't know how to defend themselves against women. Psychologically speaking, nine out of ten women will take nine out of ten men in a fight to the finish, not with direct, head-on aggression, but with guilt, shame, and blame. These are the weapons women were conditioned to use, because they've been assigned the role of victim for so long. As men we need to learn how not to be vulnerable to women when we shouldn't be.

To have a good, loving relationship with a woman, the first thing a man has to do is to develop boundaries, to stop being vulnerable to a woman's judgments about him. This may involve standing up to her and saying no to her blame. Or it may involve stepping out of the way, as in aikido. One way to establish clearer boundaries is to get away from women and spend more time with other men. My marriage has been much better since I began to recultivate my male friendships.

The second thing is to be able to stand apart, to disengage. Paradoxically, most couples don't know how *not* to be intimate, how to live with somebody while retaining their solitude and their solitary sense of self, completely invulnerable to the other person. I like to put it this way: God didn't whisper the meaning of my life in my wife's ear, or vice versa. I have to have a place inside myself where nobody goes except me.

How is being invulnerable different from being closed off, shut down, and unresponsive?

There's nothing wrong with being closed down and unresponsive if you can also be opened up, feelingful, and compassionate. There's a proper time in relationships not to feel, to withdraw into yourself. One of the most difficult things I ever have to do is to allow people near and dear to me to have their own suffering. Sometimes it's not helpful to them for me to feel their pain.

Then the third movement is to really be with another person. The three work together: standing against, standing apart, and being with. In the mode of being with another, vulnerability is a good thing. At the moment of standing against, you don't want to be vulnerable, you want to have a good set of quite appropriate defenses.

What advice do you have for men and women on being with one another? These days there seems to be a lot of suffering and confusion about how men and women can be together in an equal, mutually enriching, and non-hostile way.

Claude Levi-Strauss has a marvelous definition of myth. He says that in a given culture, myth is what teaches the appropriate distance between things. How close a father and a daughter should be, or a mother and son, or two cousins. In our culture, as I mentioned earlier, we have enormous confusion about how close men and women should be. We have a sentimental Hollywood notion that intimacy means no distance between. Two can live as easily as one. I knew couples in the old days who never spent a day or evening apart, and to whom the idea of separate vacations was horrifying. That's too close; it's symbiotic. I start off with the notion that men and women are naturally very far apart.

You see, I've given up the expectation, although probably not the hope, that a woman will understand me—or vice versa. They don't understand us. Men understand other men, but we don't really understand women. Loving is not about knowing. The more I love somebody, the more that person becomes a mystery to me, just as the more I love myself, the more I leave behind the stereotypes and realize that I'm much better and also much worse, much crueler and also much kinder, much deeper than I know myself to be. The same thing in a relationship. We should stop telling each other who we are.

That reminds me of something Kahlil Gibran said in The Prophet*: "Those who understand us enslave something in us."*

Exactly. We tend to see mystery and strangeness as dangerous, whereas in fact strangeness is the prerequisite for the continuation of all love. Instead, we've been trying to define one another all along. Men told women they didn't think and proceeded to tell them what it meant to think "like a man." We mistold them. They think differently than men. Women told men we didn't know how to feel; they said, "We'll teach you how to feel." Men's patterns of feelings are different. We have to go deeply into the mystery of our own gender and therefore allow the mystery of the other.

Second, as I mentioned earlier, we have to stop buying women's blame. There's a very negative faction within feminism that wants to blame men for everything bad since Western history began. These women curse patriarchal technology, yet they fly to conferences on airplanes, write papers on Macs, and have them published in books printed on high-tech presses denouncing the very technology they're making such abundant use of. We have to laugh at such nonsense. We created the system together.

Third, we've got to listen with compassion to the suffering of women, and to our own. This is where vulnerability comes in. Listen to women talk about their wounds, about their bitterness and anger at being demeaned and told they're second-rate, at being told that the bearing and raising of children is less important than the manufacturing of gadgets. The gynophobia and sexual debasement of women in our culture is horrendous. Men need to really hear and feel their wound.

For their part, women must hear what it means for men to have hardened themselves and to live a life of numbness for the sake of society. We didn't do this voluntarily, it was imposed upon us. Our numbness, our lack of feeling, is our historical tragedy; it's the burden we bear. If women don't understand this, they'll always be blaming us.

So a certain amount of mutual understanding needs to take place.

Enormous mutual understanding and compassion. We have to realize that the techno-economic-gender system that both men and women have conspired to create is victimizing us all. It's oppressing our psyches, destroying our ecosphere, and alienating us from one another. When both men and women feel the rage and impotence of being victims, we can begin to feel the other half of the truth—our freedom and power to change. Then we can stop wallowing in our victimhood, grieve our losses, and begin to dismantle the system together.

Susan Griffin

As feminist poet, philosopher, and social critic, Susan Griffin has investigated the ways in which the oppression of women in our society reflects a deep split in the collective psyche. By denying the natural, the instinctual, the erotic, and projecting it onto women, we have, in her view, attempted to dominate the natural world by dominating both women and nature.

Griffin's best-known work, *Woman and Nature: The Roaring Inside Her*, is a dialogue between conflicting voices, one a parody of "scientific objectivity," the other a woman's voice, feelingful, embodied, tentative at first and then slowly coming into its own power. The result is a stunning re-creation of a struggle that has characterized our civilization for millennia—and one with which we are all familiar on a personal level as well. How, we wonder, can we be fully human in a world that denies our humanity and instead demands that we be disengaged, "objective," unmoved?

In the following interview, Susan Griffin describes how a somewhat different but parallel split—between spirit and nature—informs what we have been taught to call spirituality. In its stead, she proposes a spirituality that affirms the body, the emotions, the instincts—indeed, our identity with nature. For to see that we *are* nature is, according to Griffin, the ultimate realization, which whole civilizations and social institutions have tried to obscure.

Susan Griffin

The Denial of Eros

Is there a feminist spirituality?

Yes, I think there is. But if you're going to talk about spirituality, you have to go about it in another direction. Rather than talking about "feminist spirituality," you have to recognize that what we've grown up calling spirituality in the West actually reflects the bias of the dominant culture—which, historically, has been a masculine bias—not only against women but against nature, against the physical fact of existence. This perspective is dualistic; it splits spirit and nature. The whole idea we have of spirit as something above and transcendent has been shaped by a philosophical tradition which is also intimately tied up with the oppression and denigration of women. All my philosophical work has been about showing the connection between these two things, through the issues of ecology, pornography, and now war.

Could you talk a little more about the connection between this dualistic perspective, the oppression of women, and the dominance of nature.

Well, I think we're set on the Earth with a basic life task or problem (however you wish to see it), which is that we're mortal, we age, we're subject to loss and pain and difficulty, and we're not in total control, in the sense that we're part of a larger system. There could be an avalanche or an earthquake. The economy could fail. A loved one could die. . . . There are an infinite number of cultural responses you can make to this condition, but the response of Western civilizations, certainly, has been to propose that human beings have a capacity which renders us above natural process. This capacity is associated with the divine, and we are taught to identify with the divinity which is above natural process—and which, in the most extreme case, Western civilization, is hostile to natural process. The devil is in the underworld (literally, under the earth), and God is up there in heaven.

Of course, the devil was an incarnation of Pan, the nature god.

Yes, and also an incarnation of the subconscious. Pan is associated with repressed thoughts and feelings and sexuality. But it's not possible to split off from one's natural existence. We speak of nature as if it were something outside us, but we are nature. So we create a repressed self, what I call the denied self. That's the self that "knows" with a knowledge that precedes language, a knowledge that is not the same as cerebration; it's the inescapable knowledge that we are of nature. All you have to do is be aware that you're breathing—which many people will go to great lengths to avoid.

One of the institutionalized ways this culture handles such repressed material is through projection. The culture projects those human qualities that are most associated with nature—for example, sexual feelings, or carnality in general—onto a group defined as other, whether it be black people in this country, or Jews (and more recently Arabs) in Europe, or women. So the notion that the spirit is above nature, and not emanating from and inside nature, is tied up with the oppression of women. What is natural and inherent in every human being is projected onto women.

There is also another kind of projection in which women are robbed of the spiritual qualities that are intrinsic to nature, such as self-reflection or wisdom, so that women are described as chiefly natural, according to our very reductive idea of what nature is, and as not spiritual, according to our also reductive and certainly falsely transcendent idea of spirit.

Do you think this split between spirit and nature is also true of Buddhism and the yogic traditions?

Yes, although I think Buddhism, like Christianity, has heretical sects that question the split a little more. The Buddha himself did, at the beginning. But what I find valuable in Buddhism is the meditation practice. Because whatever the doctrine says, if you're watching your breath, you're situated in your body and aware of your body. Now, certain kinds of Buddhist practice can get very severe and try to take control of the body in a way that I think reflects a pathological desire to dominate nature.

Of course, much yogic practice as well has to do with controlling the body, controlling the physical process. Pranayama, for example, is about controlling the breathing, controlling the flow of prana, and ultimately about transcending maya, the world of illusion.

Yes. What I think is interesting is, if you go back to the very beginning of any of these traditions (and this includes Judaism and Christianity), you find that they worshipped or revered the female form, which has been associated with the Earth from the very earliest times. Over time, the maternal "material" was taken farther and farther from its source, was masculinized in form, and came more and more to represent domination. Of course, there's a great deal of knowledge in yoga about the body and about material existence; otherwise, it couldn't be done.

But the question is, How is it used?

Yes, how is it used? What's the intent, what's the psychological attitude? Once a certain intent gets established, the practice itself starts to become distorting or punishing toward the body. What started out as a kind of wisdom of the body then becomes a way in which to try to dominate the body and make it fit certain patterns.

It seems you could do the same practices with two very different attitudes. You could practice yoga with the attitude that mind and body are one, with a desire to enter into and become one with the energetic process. Or you could do it as a way of separating consciousness out and divorcing yourself from physical reality.

Yes. And I imagine if you practiced with the understanding that mind and body are one, you would have certain realizations and make certain discoveries that would alter the practice, just as the practice has undoubtedly been altered over years of living with this dualism, in which physical sensation is looked at as illusion.

You were saying earlier that, as the major religions evolved, reference to or inclusion of the feminine dimension was expunged over time. In the Jewish tradition, for example, there was worship of a goddess, early on, which was eliminated. Later, there were priestesses who worked closely with the Earth forces, and these were driven out as well. And then there was the Baal Shem Tov and the Hasidic tradition, which reintroduced the feminine aspect of the divine.

Yes, and I think anytime you get someone who reintroduces the feminine, you also get someone who's anti-authoritarian. The Baal Shem Tov was definitely saying it's not doctrine that's important, it's your immediate relationship with God. And he talked about joy being more important than suffering.

What a heresy! Dancing and singing and celebrating life!

Right. Then, of course, that too became its own doctrine, and you get Hasidic sects that just go through the paces and forget the heart of the teaching. It's awfully hard to sustain any kind of non-dualistic worldview in the midst of a civilization that is so hostile to such experience. We have institutions, an entire way of life, built around dualism. In order not to be dualistic, it takes a certain kind of very interesting effort—an effort not to have so much effort, really. Because dualistic systems are filled with effort. Repression and denial take a great deal of effort.

How do you see this dualism pervading our culture?

Oh God, it's everywhere. For example, the Pentagon had this plan at one point that in case of a nuclear war in which the president died, the vice president would go up in an airplane and continue to wage the war from the sky. I immediately saw that as a kind of split self: the president, the Earth-self, dies, but the vice president, the transcendent sky-soul, continues to wage the war up in this airplane. That's a quite frightening and literal example of how we split away from the fact of death. We refuse to face the fact that the president, who is symbolically every person, will die in the event of a nuclear war.

As if the Earth could be destroyed, and somehow we could escape into the sky. As if we could extricate ourselves from the matrix.

Exactly. As if we could extricate ourselves from the matrix. Another area in which this split is reflected is in the practice of modern medicine. For example, the heroic medical approach to dying people is to extend their lives a couple of months in absolute agony. That has more to do with the doctors' need to feel control over death than with helping the patient or the family. It's really quite awful for the people involved.

There's an attempt to dominate and control the body, and a fear of natural processes.

Yes. And the way most doctors treat patients, which is patronizing and objectifying, has to do with this attempt by both the doctor and the patient to feel in control. It's very reassuring. The patient goes in and gives her power to the doctor, and the doctor pretends he has all this power over natural processes, over the body.

This is one of the ways women participate in the culture of the fathers as much as men do. We participate by identifying imaginally with the control of the people in power. If we didn't do this, we wouldn't still be oppressed.

You also see this dualism in the traditional sex roles. The man is supposed to think, make things happen in the world, build houses, mow the lawn, take charge. Whereas the woman is supposed to feel and respond to things sensually, and somehow raise children—as if raising children weren't a highly practical survival task. But this split doesn't reflect the way things actually work, even in the most traditional institutions. The split is an idealized one, and it's basically the split between culture and nature. The man, who is identified with culture, is supposed to dominate. That's the point of the whole system.

Then the question is, why did it turn out that way? And I think it's because women are mothers, so the infant is born identifying the power of nature with the woman's body.

So you think that, during birth and the nurturing period, the notion of woman as identified with nature enters the consciousness of both men and women and is somehow perpetuated.

Yes, that's right. I think that, to be able to move into adult consciousness, one needs to know that one is nature. But as a society we have been frozen and have not made this move into adult consciousness; rather, we identify woman with nature and attempt to conquer nature by dominating women. So we continue living in a state of madness that is reflected in all our social institutions.

When you talk about the exploitation of women, I think also of the tremendous exploitation of men in our society. The price men pay is enormous, though most men aren't aware of it or wouldn't be willing to admit it. Most men suffer enormously for being out of touch with their bodies, their vulnerability, their receptivity, their creativity.

Yes, I think so. I don't think anybody in the real sense of the word "wins" in this system; nobody gets to be whole if each of us can claim only one of those roles. We are all split off from parts of ourselves.

Speaking of split-off parts of ourselves, you've talked elsewhere about what you call the denial of eros, which is so pervasive in our culture. Could you say a little more about that?

Yes. Well, eros is a wild card, you know. It's constantly cracking open the heart and pulling us off in directions where we lose conscious control. Sappho writes in one of her poems, "Love shakes my heart like the wind shaking the oak tree." Eros is like that—a shudder to the whole system, an uncontrollable, unpredictable movement. Eros is also related to fecundity, to the generative, creative part of life, which we're very afraid of in this culture because it threatens our systems of defense. The fear of eros is like a fear of life itself.

Eros also includes all kinds of emotions we usually think of as negative, like anger and sadness and passion. If we're all going around trying to be so damn good all the time, we're missing out on what the emotions are meant to teach us. You get taught by your anger, you get taught by your erotic feelings. I think one of the values of meditation, vipassana especially, is that you get to feel those things and also have a look at them.

You're not necessarily caught by them.

Right, you're not caught. Reflection is a natural human capacity, and it's a way of working a little more consciously with the emotions. Emotions are very interesting because an emotion itself is always in process, it's always moving, always changing. If you don't control your anger, for example, you'll be angry for a while, and then it will move, as it must, of its nature. But if you're trying to control it, then you may make the anger into an object, into an intellectual construct, and ultimately into a way of life, and the anger becomes a replacement for actual emotions. Following on the anger in a natural progression there may be sorrow, or tenderness, or vulnerability. But in order to protect yourself from the natural play and evolution of the emotions, you may say, "Gee, this anger feels good, it feels strong, it's the right stance, I'm going to be angry all the time." You can do this with any emotion; you can say, "I'm just going to be in love all the time," or "I'm just going to be sad all the time." What we usually call being over emotional—for example, being all blustery and in a rage—isn't really being emotional at all, but rather performing on the basis of a construct, an idea we have of ourselves. We weave a story around the anger, create a scenario with ourselves as one part, then perpetuate the anger by perpetuating the scenario in our minds.

Emotions, then, are one of the conveyors of that other kind of knowledge you were taking about earlier.

Yes. In the soul (I like the word "soul," because for me it includes both body and mind) the emotions are like rivers that nourish the land; they bear wisdom. If I'm repressing a certain feeling because I'm supposed to be a good person and open and accepting of everything, I forgo that wisdom.

What about those traditions that say that the process is one of disidentification from our emotions? If we don't disidentify, then aren't we being mired in samsara, or the sins of the flesh?

You see, we don't have to disidentify from the emotions. If we just dwell with them but don't have a need to make them into a permanent identity or hang onto them for security, our emotions will disidentify from us. They have other places to go; they have a very short half-life.

Arnold Mindell

When I first met Jungian analyst Arnold Mindell several years ago, I thought he might be a bit crazy. As I attempted to interview him over tea, he zigzagged from one topic to another, laughed uproariously, asked me unsettling questions, and otherwise refused to behave like the usual celebrity interviewee. Yet it was not his mercurial hijinks that threw me off guard; it was his warmth, his ingenuous, childlike affection. This strange fellow acted as if he'd known me all his life. Could I be in the presence of some holy Sufi fool, I wondered?

As I've spent time with him over the years, I've come to appreciate the method (and the wisdom) in Mindell's madness. In fact, he is a psychologist with impeccable credentials, including experience as a training analyst at the Jung Institute in Zurich. He is also author of half a dozen books and founder of his own training center, the Research Society for Process Oriented Psychology. What he has added to Jung's understanding of unconscious process is the notion of the "dreambody"—the unconscious as an active agent constantly expressing itself in our lives.

Rather than a repository of archetypes, as Jung had suggested, the unconscious, or dreambody, according to Mindell, is a dynamic, flowing continuum of which archetypes are only "snapshots." Dreams, physical symptoms, relationships, accidents, altered states of consciousness—all are manifestations of the dreambody in action.

In particular, Mindell has developed a complex methodology for revealing the deeper meaning of bodily processes: feelings, pains, habitual gestures, even chronic illnesses. Whereas some therapies or meditation techniques attempt to eliminate or ignore these processes, especially the ones considered negative or undesirable, Mindell's approach is to amplify and follow them until they reveal their hidden message. Indeed, his belief in the underlying meaning of all things human has given him the courage to work successfully with situations and states of mind that most therapists would consider unworkable, including intense interpersonal conflict, violent convulsions, catatonia, even mental retardation and coma. Two of his books, *Coma: Key to Awakening* and *City Shadows: Psychological Interventions in Psychiatry*, feature extraordinary case examples of this work.

A short, wiry man with a mischievous smile, Mindell brings to a client's process the energy and attentiveness of a martial arts master, the curiosity of a scientist, and the empathy of an intimate friend. During a demonstration recently, I watched as he deftly took one woman from talk about her symptom—frequent urination—through a series of interactive, dancelike movements to a visionary experience in a scant 20 minutes. Since most of us in the West, according to Mindell, have suppressed our innate tendency to express ourselves in movement, his work with clients often shifts from words to kinesthetic expression. The directors of California's famed Esalen Institute were so impressed with process-oriented psychology that they hired Mindell to teach it to their staff.

The story of Mindell's initiation into the world of Jungian psychology reads like a chapter from one of his own books on dreambody phenomena. After studying both languages and science in college, Mindell, a native of New York State, did graduate work in physics at M.I.T. and then transferred to the Ph.D. program at the University of Zurich. He soon found physics "too dry," however, and when he began having "wild dreams," a fellow student referred him to the "old witch" of Zurich, who turned out to be Marie-Louise von Franz, one of Jung's foremost successors and an expert in dream interpretation. As it happened, Jung had died just a few days earlier, intimating, on his deathbed, that the next step in Jungian psychology would be to explore its connection with physics!

Mindell and von Franz explored the problem of synchronicity together, and Mindell ended up getting a Ph.D. in psychology rather than physics and an analyst's diploma from the Jung Institute. Although he was fascinated by Jung's teachings (and still reminds people that his work is just a continuation of Jung's), he brought his scientist's eye for detail and demand for concrete evidence to bear on the therapeutic process. "Just talking about the unconscious wasn't that interesting to me," he says. "I had to see how it operated in real, living people. That's how I eventually got into bodywork. I wanted to see how dreams lived in the body." In particular, his work with terminally ill patients "initiated me into modes of nonverbal communication whose significance I otherwise would have overlooked."

Like the Taoist philosophers he is fond of referring to, Mindell believes that what happens to us in each moment is exactly what was meant to happen. Our task is to learn to follow this process as it unfolds and thereby help it to reveal its deeper significance. A physical symptom, for example, may force us to deal with a relationship issue, get us in touch with a mythological figure, resolve an old childhood dream, or guide us into a profound meditative state. "I think we're doing what spiritual practices are trying to do as well," Mindell contends. "Long ago I dreamed that the Buddha said that if process work had been available in his day, he would have used it, because it's an express train to the same spot."

Whether or not process work leads to enlightenment, it is clearly a powerful therapeutic approach whose theoretical underpinnings have more in common with the world's spiritual traditions than with conventional Western psychology. In the following interview, conducted on two separate occasions in conference hotel rooms, Arny Mindell discusses the philosophy and practice of process-oriented psychology.

Arnold Mindell

Field of Dreams

Arny, in your work as a Jungian analyst, you discovered that the unconscious, the "dreambody," manifests not only through dreams but also through other channels. Could you say a little about those channels and what they signify.

When you talk about the unconscious "manifesting itself through dreams," I think to myself that the unconscious itself is a dreaming process; it's a flow or a river. Dreams are only snapshots of the river. What really began to fascinate me was the dreaming process behind those dreams.

Whereas traditional Jungians generally become fixated on the photograph.

Yes. Many Jungians look at the river and talk about archetypes, and then they start to do this funny thing. They say, "Well, if you analyze and interpret one archetype, it has a tendency to flow into another archetype. Way down deep there is a smudging of archetypes." What they're really saying is that there's a flowing or dreaming process at the bottom of it all.

This process manifests itself in many different ways, depending on the channel in which we perceive it. One of the channels is proprioception—you feel things inside your body in terms of temperatures, pressures, pains, aches, joys, sexual stimulation, and so forth. Or you experience things in terms of visual imagery, or in terms of auditory phenomena, like voices, or in terms of movement—the way you trip over your shoelaces or make certain kinds of gestures—or even in terms of relationship processes. Other people can act as sensory channels for you; you can experience yourself in terms of the behavior of others. And the process also manifests through extrasensory or parapsychological channels: The trees do things; the sky speaks to us. This is the channel of the American Indians, you might say. The unconscious has many ways of manifesting itself.

You say that other people in my life are part of my dreaming process. What do you mean by that?

I mean that we all have a tendency to "dream up" other people to behave like our dream figures. This causes us to project parts of ourselves onto such people, and it also causes us to choose them as partners so we can work things out with them. When I say, "So-and-so feels this or that," I may actually be saying that *I* feel this or that, though I haven't yet identified this person as a channel of awareness in myself.

How do you work with the different channels? For example, say a person comes in who is troubled by a very severe inner critic that hounds her all the time.

First of all, the most important thing in working with people is the skill with which you use the other skills, what I call the meta-skill. This is the feeling or attitude you have about yourself and others. If you have a compassionate attitude, that in itself generates what you do.

So you don't simply take some technique and apply it. Rather, it comes from within you in the context of love and caring toward others.

That's right. When you have a compassionate attitude toward people, you automatically start picking up their feedback and responding to it. Someone with a severe inner critic may start out by saying, "I'm hearing inner criticism all the time." So I might say, "Do you want to listen to it right now?" If she says, "No, I hate it. I hear it all the time," I might respond to her negative feedback by saying, "OK, then let's talk about something else." After a while, she may come back to the criticism, and I'll again suggest going into it. If she gives me positive feedback at this point, I'll have her listen to the inner critic for a while, asking who it is, whether it's a man or a woman, her mother or her husband or her boss, etc.

Then she might say, "Oh, my stomach hurts." Now she's switched to the proprioceptive channel. "What does that feel like?" I might ask. "Well, it feels bad," she says, making a fist at the same time. So we focus on the fist, which is a kinesthetic or movement expression of the same process. Then I might have her amplify the fist by making a muscle in her bicep, tightening her neck, and tensing her face. Suddenly she says, "Now I look like my father." "What does he look like?" I ask. "He looks like you!" At this point, I would probably say, "Can't we take this inward? Does it have to be projected outward? Are you really criticizing me? I think you just don't like me."

Now you're in the relationship channel.

Exactly. This is what I call "dreaming up," which is relationship work. Then as a therapist I have to look inside myself and see whether a part of me isn't in fact critical of her. There may be, in which case I need to recognize and talk about that part. We may go back and forth until the person realizes that I'm not like her father, but the fatherlike part is in her.

You have to be quite genuine in these interactions, and aware at many levels—of what's going on inside you, in the client, and in the environment as well.

Exactly. I have to be aware of the whole process, because I'm part of the process too.

What you're referring to here, if I'm not mistaken, is what you call the "dream field," in which people and objects take on the qualities of our dreaming process.

Yes. We dream up the world around us to behave like our own dream field. All these different parts and roles are present in each of us and in the environment. When we dream something up, we call forth a certain part to play a role in our own evolutionary process. For example, if I lack awareness of the shy part of myself, I may dream you up to represent that part, to balance my one-sidedness, and you may dream me up to represent the bold part of you. Then we start experiencing one another as dream figures, as opposites within ourselves. Just by being one-sided or unconscious, we constellate dream fields.

Freudians might say that you were "transferring" certain qualities of your mother or father onto someone else. Jungians might talk about projecting an archetype.

Yes, those are just different ways of talking about the same thing, except that sometimes things happen synchronistically that can't be explained in terms of simple projection. For example, you dream that a huge bird speaks to you, and the next day you're walking down the street and for the first time in your life a large bird actually bumps into you. This is not something you can talk about in terms of simple projection. The world sometimes does literally behave as if it were a sensory channel, as if it were a part of your dreaming field.

We often call such occurrences coincidences, whereas you're suggesting they have meaning.

Yes. You see, most people think like physicists. They believe that unpredictable occurrences are just coincidence or chance. But psychologists and spiritually oriented people realize that the unpredictable, the event that happens only once, is itself very meaningful.

For example, a woman I once worked with had a very sharp pain in her right breast. She was living in Los Angeles at the time, and she discovered later that exactly at the moment she had that pain, her sister in New York died of breast cancer. She herself eventually developed cancer in that breast. So one-time occurrences can be very important.

What you're proposing has correspondences with Eastern philosophy. For example, the I Ching *is very much concerned with one-time occurrences that happen simultaneously. The idea is that there's a field of meaning, and that things that happen at the same moment are somehow related in a meaningful way.*

Exactly. That's how the world behaves as a channel. There's really nothing new in what I'm saying. These ideas are implicit, for example, in Taoism. You could say I'm just attempting to learn how to follow the Tao, not just talk about it.

Everyone is a Toaist at heart. Everyone would like to follow nature, but we don't have enough tools yet to put the philosophy into practice. All over the world—for example, we've just been working in the African bush—people say they believe in human nature. But as soon as someone gets sick, they fight the illness, rather than trying to find the meaning or purpose behind it. I think they just don't know how yet.

Say a little more about how you see process work as a kind of Taoism.

Taoism for me means becoming aware of and following what's actually happening—both the intentional and the unintentional, the conscious and the unconscious. Process-oriented psychology is simply a way of doing that.

Most of us can get into harmony with our conscious process, but we don't seem to have the tools to harmonize with our unconscious process. Process-oriented psychology, then, offers a method for coming into harmony with the whole process, both conscious and unconscious.

That's right. Even present-day Taoists are correcting the body all the time. They say they are trying to get into the Tao by balancing the body. But why balance it? Why not go with the Tao of no-balance? In the *I Ching* there are conflict hexagrams as well as stagnation hexagrams. The Tao has moments of conflict as well as moments of harmony. Why not get into those too?

In other words, why not allow the conflict to be there, work with it as it is, allow it to unfold.

That's right. I think, for example, of a woman who came to a seminar we were giving and said she had ruptured discs in her back. She had to be carried in; she was virtually paralyzed. She wondered how we could possibly work with her. We said, "Let's just follow nature. The Way will direct us. Let's see where it takes us." She began to follow her pains and work with her breathing and her body. Very soon she began to move spontaneously. While she was moving, she said, "What shall I do next?" I said, "Let's follow what's actually happening to you." So we followed her breathing, and as I pressed my hands lightly on her ribcage, she suddenly said, "I feel like moving in strange directions." I said, "Well, do it." I helped her to follow her body by using my hands to sculpt it in the directions it was already moving, following her body signals. Pretty soon, of all the impossible things, she began to bend over backwards in the yoga pose called the Bridge!

For somebody with ruptured discs, this is miraculous. "It hurts," she said, "but for some reason, this time it feels good." I didn't know what to suggest to her, so I said, "Follow what feels right." She kept going backwards and finally said, "My God, I'm being crucified and uplifted." She started to cry, and she had a powerful religious experience. She stayed there for the longest time, arched over backwards in a sort of half bridge position, breathing deeply. Then she bent forward, sat up normally again, and thanked me.

"Does this remind you of a childhood dream?" I asked her. She said the first thing she could remember was that people in UFOs were coming to uplift her. The process of being uplifted was trying all these years to happen to her, and it was manifesting itself in her back. This is an example of following the Tao of the moment.

What about her back?

Her back felt immediately better. She sat up without help or support, stood up, smiled, and walked around. She was glowing—something more important than her backache had happened to her.

I don't know whether the changes held. But I don't consider that as important as the increased awareness, which is what we're working toward. We're not trying to heal people.

But doesn't "psychotherapist" mean "one who heals the psyche"? How do you conceptualize the healing process?

The word "healing" implies that somebody is sick. I don't usually go along with that metaphor anymore. If people insist on seeing themselves as sick, I appreciate their way of looking at things, and I may even try to heal them. But I consider healing much too limited a concept. I prefer to see disease as a dream trying to come to consciousness. When a person goes into the experience, it's almost never illness, but some intense process trying to happen.

The Vietnamese Buddhist teacher Thich Nhat Hanh says that true understanding comes from putting yourself inside the river. Previous knowledge is a block to understanding. If you think you're sick, that's fine, but it's a block to real understanding. Who knows if you're sick? Who knows what's really happening to you?

What you're saying, then, is that, despite our own little ideas of how we want things to be, underneath it all, there's this deeper, more universal process needing to happen, through us and through the world. This is what you call the "dreambody."

Yes, exactly.

Or it could be called the Tao, or God. All we need to do is tune in.

Yes. There's really nothing to it. I sometimes feel guilty that I don't do more. I can't believe that these incredible experiences emerge from people as a result of my doing so little. They're just waiting to happen; all we have to do is mother them a little.

That's where the technique comes in.

Yes, the know-how, the awareness. It's like a spiritual practice in the sense that you need to be aware of what's happening and ready to welcome rather than reject it.

What you're doing sounds like more than just therapy. Underneath it all there's a spiritual dimension.

Yes. The spiritual component is the belief in the flow of our perceptions. After all, what else is there? Our perceptions are the only reality we know. If we believe other people's perceptions instead of our own, we've disavowed ourselves, and pretty soon we've stopped loving ourselves too. But if we value our perceptions and follow them, we can eventually become whole. This is very different from what we usually do. Everyone says we should believe in our perceptions, but very few actually do.

Inherent in what you're saying, it seems, is a critique not only of conventional psychotherapy, but also of many spiritual practices. Could you say a little more about this.

Most traditional spiritual practices are behavioral programs. They teach you to behave in a certain way and to see certain kinds of perceptions as wrong or insignificant. For example, if you experience pain, you're supposed to let it go or ignore it. Whereas if you really believe in your perceptions, you don't say, "This is *just* my body," but rather, "This is *my* body, and it's hurting. I notice my tendency to ignore my pain, but it doesn't help. Maybe my body is wise. Maybe it has something to teach me."

Whereas spiritual practices may teach us to say, "This is only my body. What's really important is the spirit."

Yes. When you do that, you're implicitly devaluing certain channels—in this case, proprioception. I think the better teachers, the wiser students, don't make this mistake. But if you're not taught to value all your perceptions, then spiritual practice isn't doing what it purports to do, which is to teach you to open to and love the whole human being. There's a lack of heartfulness. With some spiritual teachers and groups, you may feel that part of you is accepted but a whole other part isn't.

Also, if you're a good ecologist, you have to wonder where your signals and processes—the parts of you seeking expression—go when you disavow or let go of them. We used to think that negativity just went out into the universe, or the gods digested it, or something like that. Now we know that the world is very small, and the negativity doesn't just disappear. It goes into your body, into a less tractable process, maybe a cellular or metabolic or cancerlike process. Or it goes into your partner, who hates you. Or it goes into accidents on the street corner or into the collective, for you and me to pick up. Devaluing certain perceptions and just letting them go is like tossing wastepaper onto the street. Somebody has to clean it up eventually.

Spiritual practices talk a lot about compassion, but compassion also means having compassion toward all your perceptions, even the unhappy or unfortunate ones, and trying to process them.

For example, what if you're really furious with your partner? If you act nice and pretend not to be angry, your partner will pick up the anger anyway. Whereas if you work with the signals of that fury, it can carry you through to another place.

I'm thinking of a particular couple I worked with recently. He was always sleeping with someone else, and she was furious about it but didn't say so. As they sat together, her eyes were wide open. So I said to her, "When you open your eyes like that, what is it about?"

She stared at him and said, "I'm furious with you!" She was trying to express the energy of anger through her eyes. Naturally, his eyes opened wide too, and they were both absolutely furious with one another.

She said, "I hate you for sleeping with all these other women."

He said, "Well, you're a good-for-nothing so-and-so."

Then her voice went down. So I said, "Follow that."

"I was just trying to get angry," she said.

"OK," I said. "If you're angry, continue." She continued for a moment, but her voice started getting hoarse.

"I think you should follow the de-escalating signal," I said. "What happens now?"

"Now I feel very quiet," she said. Then he quieted down too, and the two of them sat together in stillness. These are not meditators, but they started to meditate, and finally he started to cry.

"What was that?" I asked.

"I never knew I could be with her in utter silence like this. It's very beautiful," he said. And they embraced.

The whole process took six or seven minutes. It's an example of following the Tao of the moment as a way to the greater relationship. The trouble is, just as people get detached from one signal, they get attached to another. As soon as they're free to be furious, they get stuck in their fury and can't move on to anything else.

How do you understand the process of individual growth or transformation?

There seem to be a number of different phases or stages to the evolution of consciousness. There's a stage of analytical awareness, in which you look inside yourself, notice different aspects, have some insights, and start to think about them. At this point you might try to figure things out or apply a program to yourself; you might start meditating or get into Jungian analysis or some other form of talk therapy.

Then there is what I call the Buddhist stage, in which you notice things and let them go through you. Here you develop what the Buddhists call the witness consciousness. After you've done this for a long time, you start noticing that many of the thoughts and emotions don't really go through, they get stuck. Then you might consider a process-oriented stage, where you notice things arising, but, instead of letting them go, you get on top of them and ride them, helping them pass through more rapidly by amplifying or intensifying them.

After that, there is still a further stage, in which you realize that everything you're doing is just a phase, and that the different methods work fine for different times in your life, depending on what is happening to you in a given moment. This, I think, is one of the highest stages.

There's a sense in what you're saying that transformation is ongoing; it isn't necessarily just a one-time occurrence.

Transformation continues right up until the very last heartbeat. I've seen this in working with people in comatose states.

How do you work with people in coma? I mean, by all standards they're impossible to communicate with.

Yes, you can't awaken them by ordinary means. But from my experience I now know that people in comatose states do want to wake up. The trouble is that the people around them don't know how to communicate with them. A heartful helper may meditate or hold their hand. But that is usually insufficient. If you follow their breathing and amplify the noises they're making, almost all of them will awaken, except those that have had severe structural brain damage, where the muscles no longer work properly. Even among those people, the majority will open their eyes, focus, and give you feedback. Especially people in metabolic comas— those that are comatose because of chemical changes in the blood—awaken and go through the most incredible stories.

So you actually are able, in most cases, to communicate with these people and arouse them to the point of waking up?

Yes. Take John, for example, a black man I mention in my book. He had been lying in a hospital in coma for six months, rasping and making lots of noise and waking up all the other patients. I went to see him and made noises with him while gently squeezing his hand. After about ten minutes, he opened his eyes and said, "You saw that too?" I said, "I did see it. What do you see?"

"A big white ship is a-comin' for John!"

"Are you going to take it?" I asked.

"Not me," he yelled. "I'm not gettin' on that ship."

"Why not?" I asked.

"That ship's goin' on vacation. I gotta get up in the morning and go to work."

John had worked hard all his life and was now in his 80s. His cancer had reduced him to a bag of bones. He was stuck at the end of life because he couldn't allow himself to go on vacation. So I said to him, "Well, getting up in the morning and going to work sounds good to me. But before we do it, let's check the ship out. Take a look inside and see who's driving that ship." So he went down into the ship and said with great excitement, "Whew! There's angels down there driving that ship."

"Do you want to find out where it's going?" I asked.

He went inside again and turned his eyes to the right, apparently listening to something, and said, "That ship is a-goin' to Bermuda."

"Well, what's it cost?" I said, knowing that he was a practical guy. After a minute he said, "It don't cost nothin'."

"Think about it," I said. "Ever have a vacation?"

"I never had a vacation. Never. I've been workin' and workin' and workin'."

"Well, think about it. Make your choice."

Finally, he said, "I'm goin' on vacation! It don't cost nothin', and it's goin' to Bermuda."

I said, "Chances are, if you don't like it, maybe it'll turn around and come back."

"Yeah. I can always get off that ship."

"You do what you want," I said. "I'll trust your judgment. I'm busy and have to go see somebody else now." So he closed his eyes and that was it. When we came back 30 minutes later he had died. He'd gone to Bermuda.

That's a beautiful story.

Yes, it is. I've been doing this for almost 15 years, but I never mentioned these stories to anybody until my wife, Amy, started coming with me to the hospital. I thought nobody would believe me. Elisabeth Kübler-Ross said she believed me, but she had never seen it herself. People don't usually work with comatose states.

I had a similar experience with my own mother. She'd had a stroke and gone into a coma, and she wasn't supposed to be able to talk. I worked with her breathing, and out of the rasping she started to make noises, and then—a song! [Hums melody of "Row, Row, Row Your Boat"] We began to sing together [sings], and I sang the words because she couldn't move her mouth very well. When we got to the end of the first verse, my mother roared out, "Life is but a dream!"

I could hardly believe it! "But everybody thought you were comatose," I said. "I don't know what you're talking about," she replied. "Let's call up all the relatives," I said, "and let's sing." And she did sing "Life is but a dream" to all her relatives before she died.

Joan Borysenko

As I drive to the airport to pick up Joan Borysenko, I find myself idly reading the billboards. One in particular attracts my attention: an enormous bottle of cognac with the slogan "Not actual size (too bad)." Hmmm. Several minutes later another catches my eye: a sporty imported car with the words "Car red. Knuckles white."

On the drive back, I mention the billboards to Joan. Could this be a trend? I muse.

"Isn't it amazing how many ads appeal to money, sex, power, and fear?" she agrees. "I wonder if anyone has ever done a market survey to determine how many automobiles they could sell by appealing to our nurturing instincts, or to our desire for bonding."

The reply, I would soon discover, is vintage Borysenko, revealing, as it does, her proclivity not only to see the source of our malaise as a culture, but also to offer positive alternatives that bring out the best in us.

Take Borysenko's first book, *Minding the Body, Mending the Mind.* A guide to stress reduction that took both publisher and author by surprise when it made the *New York Times* Bestseller List in 1987, it touts the benefits of hatha yoga, deep breathing, mindfulness meditation, and positive thinking in breaking what she calls the anxiety cycle and helping people regain control of their emotions—and their lives. Certainly an unusual first book for a Harvard-trained research scientist with a Ph.D. in anatomy and cellular biology. But Borysenko is more than a skilled researcher and an articulate teacher—she is a fervent practitioner of the disciplines she preaches, whose own lessons in stress-reduction have been personal and hard-won.

"When I was 24 and working on my doctoral dissertation at the Harvard Medical School," she writes in *Minding the Body*, "I was living on coffee and cigarettes, broke and tired, trying to cope with a troubled marriage and an infant son for whom I had far too little time. . . . I was also a physical wreck. Troubled by migraines all my life, I found in college that the intense competition had added crippling stomach pains and vomiting to my list of psychosomatic illnesses." In graduate school she developed high blood pressure, panic attacks, and fainting spells.

Conventional medicine repeatedly failed to offer her any relief, and finally, at the urging of a friend, she turned to meditation—an unusual "course of treatment" back in the 1960s. Within six month all her symptoms had disappeared. Soon Borysenko was practicing yoga, and by the time she had finished graduate studies and become an assistant professor at Tufts Medical School, the "best part of [her] week" had become the lunch-hour yoga classes she taught to colleagues and students.

Another turning point in Borysenko's life came when her father contracted leukemia and died of the side effects of his treatment. "The doctors didn't care about him as a person at all," she recalls. "They only cared about his white blood cell count. There I was, a cancer cell biologist, and yet I felt so helpless and disempowered. There was no one there to advocate for us, no cancer support groups, no mind-body medicine."

Devastated and disillusioned, Borysenko vowed to find a way to help others who, like herself and her family, suffered from the insensitivity of an approach to medicine that focuses exclusively on the body, and ignores the whole person. Shortly after, in 1978, she left her career in the laboratory to do a postdoctoral fellowship with Herbert Benson, M.D. at Harvard. Benson, author of *The Relaxation Response*, a groundbreaking popular book on meditation and stress-reduction, was a pioneer in the fledgling discipline of behavioral medicine, which studies the physiological responses that mediate the mind's effect on the body.

In 1981, after several years of collaboration, Borysenko teamed up with Benson and an Israeli psychiatrist, Dr. Ilan Kutz, to found the Mind/Body Clinic at New England Deaconess Hospital, Harvard Medical School. There they offered stress-management groups that featured meditation and hatha yoga and were designed to help participants alleviate a variety of stress-related conditions, including headaches, hypertension, cardiac arrhythmias, digestive disorders, and chronic pain. The program, on which *Minding the Body* is based, was so successful that it has served as a model for similar programs around the country. Director of the clinic since its inception, Borysenko left a few years ago to offer independent consultations for businesses and hospitals.

The area of behavioral medicine that has particularly concerned Borysenko over the years—indeed, one in which she is considered a pioneer—is psychoneuroimmunology, the study of the mind's effect on the immune system. Catapulted to public attention over a decade ago by the cancer work of O. Carl Simington, psychoneuroimmunology has proven beyond doubt that what we think and feel does more than affect the tension level in the body—it has a direct and measurable impact on our resistance to disease. According to researchers, even individual white blood cells have receptor sites for chemicals released by the brain!

Despite the profound effect meditation and yoga were having on the lives of her patients, however, Borysenko was discovering that in some cases, even when coupled with psychotherapy, these techniques were not sufficient to alleviate chronic, stress-related conditions. "Take two meditations and call me in the morning' is a typical joke in behavioral medicine circles," she laughs. "But if all we're doing is treating the symptoms with a bunch of techniques, we're not going deep enough, to the cause of the problem."

The "cause of the problem" is the topic of Borysenko's second book, *Guilt is the Teacher, Love is the Lesson.* In conversations with patients who did not respond to the clinic program or to subsequent psychotherapy, Borysenko discovered that the techniques were not reaching these people's deeply held negative beliefs about themselves and their world. Many saw the universe as a hostile place and themselves as worthless creatures who deserved to be punished—beliefs based, in many cases, on childhood experiences of shame and abuse. In her book, and in the present interview, she argues that only a spiritual awakening can uproot these deeply held beliefs and transform what she calls spiritual pessimism into spiritual optimism and love.

As we settle down in my living room on an unseasonably warm winter afternoon, Joan Borysenko and I chat about our children, a favorite topic of mine in the few years since I've become a stepparent. She is a small woman with considerable poise who speaks with the calm of a meditator and the precision and measured cadence of a seasoned scientist and teacher. Since her children are mostly grown and mine are still in grade school, I'm hoping to catch a few pointers before our interview begins. And I'm not disappointed. Indeed, it soon becomes clear that Borysenko the mother has given to her children the very qualities that Borysenko the author recommends to her readers: respect for the authentic self and trust that the best in the individual will emerge. With parents like this one, I find myself thinking, none of us would ever have grown up to be pessimists.

Joan Borysenko

Love is the Lesson

Conventional medicine generally attempts to heal the body; more holistic approaches address both the body and the mind. In your second book especially, you seem to expand the domain of healing from the body-mind to the whole person, including the spiritual dimension.

You're right. Psychology and medicine in this country don't have a place for the spiritual, for basic questions of meaning such as Who am I? or What is human life? After all, what can a person's belief system possibly have to do with their defense mechanisms, for instance, or their high blood pressure?

As I began to listen to the stories of more and more patients, however, I began to have a very different point of view. For example, I had one patient for a number of years who had intense migraine headaches. Because I had migraines myself, I'm always interested in other people with this condition. Almost everyone who learns meditation has substantial reduction in both the frequency and the intensity of their migraines. This guy, whom I'll call Mike, was highly motivated. He attended the program at the Mind-Body Clinic, he meditated twice a day, and after 10 weeks he hadn't improved at all. I was quite surprised. As I talked with him, I could see that there were some difficulties in his marriage, so I suggested that he get into psychotherapy.

About three years later, he returned to see me. His therapy had gone well, he was still meditating, he had become a vegetarian and a runner, his health habits were excellent, and his headaches hadn't eased one bit. Having covered everything else, I asked him, "What do you think the meaning of life is?" First he said he didn't know. Then he went back to his early religious training. He had been brought up as a Christian whose parents believed in a punitive, fire-and-brimstone God who was going to get you in the end. That never sat right with him, and as soon as he left for college he stopped going to church. But, as they say, you can leave the church, but does the early religious conditioning ever leave you? Not, I think, unless you pay close attention to it.

I questioned him further. "You say you don't believe in such a deity now, but what do you believe in?" As it unfolded, his idea of a higher power was a malevolent Santa Claus up there with a note card watching everything he did and passing judgment. At some point he figured it would all even out because his life had been no rockier than anyone else's. But every time circumstances went against him, he believed he was being punished for his sins.

Martin Seligman, a psychologist at the University of Pennsylvania, has written a great deal about psychological pessimism. According to Seligman, psychological pessimists make three attributions when a "bad event" occurs: internal, global, and stable. Let's say you're a student who has just failed an algebra exam. If you're a psychological pessimist, you might say, "It's all my fault (internal). I'm a bad student, I mess up everything I do (global). And I'm always going to be like this (stable)." It's not just that you failed the exam because you had too many courses this term, or because the teacher wasn't that good, or because you hate algebra. It's because you're a hopeless good-for-nothing who is never going to change. You have this pervasive sense of what I've come to call unhealthy guilt. No matter what you do, it's never good enough. In my new book, *Guilt Is the Teacher, Love Is the Lesson*, I look at how we become psychological pessimists. But Mike was more than a psychological pessimist, he was a spiritual pessimist, someone who believes, "I mess up everything I do, and furthermore God is going to get me for it."

So the attribution is not only global, it's universal.

It's even going to follow you into the afterlife! That's very frightening.

One very interesting study looked at 100 Catholics, all of whom had the same religious background and learned the same catechism. Some of them viewed the divine as merciful, compassionate, and loving, and others viewed the divine as judgmental, punitive, and full of retribution. You can find evidence for both views in the Bible, and people, it seems, will pick and choose; they'll see what they want to see. We do this with all our reading.

Do you suppose these people had an innate disposition to see things one way or another?

Their view of themselves correlated entirely with self-esteem. The higher the view they had of themselves, the more they saw God as loving. The lower their self-esteem, the more self-punitive they were, the more they projected a God in their own image.

The question then might be, Which came first, the low self-esteem or the negative image of God?

My sense is that it was the low self-esteem. Children as they grow can't tell the difference between one authority figure and another. If your parents see the best in you, honor the Self in you, and seek always to respect you as a human being, correcting your mistakes from a sense of love and trust and worthiness, then the idea you'll have of other authority figures, including God, will follow suit. In fact, however, research indicates that as many as 90 percent of us come from "dysfunctional families" where we don't get the love and respect we need. It's not surprising, then, that the majority of people create the idea of a punitive divinity.

This brings us back to stress and stress-related illness, where questions of meaning are of primary importance. Someone once asked Albert Einstein, "What is the most important question that we as human beings have to answer?" Einstein said, "It's simple: Is the universe a friendly place or not?" Now, we know for sure that bad things happen: people get sick and die, children starve, volcanoes erupt. In spite of that, many people believe in the sacred mystery of things. They believe that the force of love is operative and that, despite the uncertainty, we can still live rewarding, loving, happy lives. These people are spiritual optimists. Whereas if you're worried all the time that the world is an unsafe place or that you're being punished for your sins, it doesn't matter how much psychotherapy you do, or how much insight you have, or how much yoga or meditation you practice.

I once appeared on a talk show in Denver, and the host asked people to call in with their greatest fears. One man said his greatest fear was going to hell. I asked him what he had done. He said that in fact he had tried to live a pious life, but he knew that only great saints like Mother Teresa went to heaven. Do you think a course in stress management is going to help a person like that?

What does help someone like that, if psychotherapy and stress management don't? Many psychologists suggest that the predisposition to see the world as a negative, hostile place is learned very early, possibly even in the womb. How does one change in a radical way the experiences of early childhood?

First of all, I think one has to become conscious of them. Most of us don't give much thought to the meaning of things. For some people, their religious upbringing has been a bridge to the best in themselves and in other people. For other people, like myself, their religious tradition has been neither helpful nor injurious. But then there is a whole cadre of people out there who were damaged by their religious upbringing. Often they have turned off to it and, like our friend with the migraines, said, "This is a pile of nonsense. I have no interest in it whatsoever." But it hasn't gone away. So the first task is to bring our awareness to what is going on inside us.

How does one come to this kind of awareness?

Often one comes to it when one gets ill. When people get cancer or AIDS, for example, they generally have a theory or fantasy about why they got the disease. They may believe they're being punished for not being pure enough or for thinking incorrectly. Many have been quick to embrace the new age idea of illness as metaphor and use it not as a charge to become responsible and self-aware, but as a way of blaming themselves and reinforcing their spiritual pessimism. It's true, of course, that illness often points out to us a dysfunctional way of relating to the world. But that doesn't necessarily mean we should blame ourselves. Is illness a metaphor? I think the answer is yes, no, and maybe. Even Freud said that sometimes a cigar is just a cigar.

A woman once came to me with a pain in her shoulder and one of Louise Hay's books under her arm. She had decided that she had the pain because she was afraid to reach out and take what she wanted. I picked up her purse. It must have weighed 15 or 20 pounds. I said, "Why don't you carry a lighter purse and see what happens to your shoulder pain?" Needless to say, it went away. Her shoulder pain wasn't a metaphor, it was a 15-pound purse. Sometimes we miss the most obvious things. Someone who tends to feel guilty, who fears that they're not worthy or lovable enough, is always going to point the finger of blame at themselves when it comes to illness.

Once we've become aware of our beliefs, what next?

For one thing, there is a growing groundswell of support for spiritual optimism, even in the Judeo-Christian tradition. Then I also believe we're undergoing what Willis Harman has called a global mind change, from a metaphysic in which consciousness is seen as an attribute of the physical brain, to a metaphysic in which consciousness is primary and matter is derivative of consciousness. Once you've decided that consciousness is located in the brain, you have to conclude that consciousness ceases when the brain dies and that one person's thought cannot possibly affect another person at a distance. But Larry Dossey, in his new book *Recovering the Soul*, makes the case that consciousness is nonlocal and can affect our health in a nonlocal way, that is, my thoughts can affect you at a distance in a way that is good for your health.

If you talk to enough physicians, as I do, you hear a lot of very interesting stories about cures that couldn't possibly have happened. For example, on television a few months ago there was the story of a man who went hunting, fell out of a tree, shot himself through the groin, and bled out before his hunting partners could find him. When they finally got him to the hospital, his heart had stopped and he was brain dead. For whatever reason, they resuscitated him anyway and put him on a respirator, although he was comatose and by all scientific parameters should have remained a vegetable for the rest of his life. But his mother never believed he was going to die. She brought in her prayer group, and they prayed for him constantly. Four or five weeks later, he opened up his eyes and started to talk. Nothing in medical science could explain a case like this. The fact is, there are many cases of this sort.

In my book I cite a well-known study by Randolph Byrd that made quite a splash a couple of years ago. Byrd was a cardiologist at San

Francisco General Hospital who decided to do a study on the efficacy of prayer. He had 500 patients admitted to the coronary intensive care unit, either for heart attack or to rule out heart attack, and he had them randomly assigned to a prayed-for and a not-prayed-for group. It was the pinnacle of controlled scientific research: a randomized double-blind study. None of the staff knew who was in which group so they couldn't preferentially give care to one group and not the other, and the subjects were chosen at random, so factors like sex, age, health, and demographics would balance out. Then he farmed out their names to prayer groups of various denominations around the country.

When they broke the code at the end of the study, they found that indeed the prayed-for patients did significantly better on a number of measures. They got fewer infections, needed fewer antibiotics, got out of the hospital sooner. No one in the prayed-for group needed a respirator, whereas 16 or 17 of the others did. The differences were so significant that if prayer had been a drug, there would have been a run on the market for it. One well-known debunker of similar studies could find absolutely nothing wrong with this one. "Now I can truly say," he wrote, "that physicians should take out their pads and write prescriptions for prayer." There is no way to explain these results in terms of a brain generating consciousness in the body. The only way to explain it is that somehow the thoughts of one person can affect another person at a distance. Of course, for most of us this is just common sense.

But science seems to lag behind common sense.

It often does. Studies done by Andrew Greeley at the University of Chicago indicate that many American have had experiences of nonlocal consciousness. Nearly one-third report having had visions, half have contacted a dead loved one, two-thirds have experienced ESP, and a remarkable 35 percent report having had a mystical experience in which they were lifted out of themselves by a "powerful, spiritual force." While science is trying to make a case for nonlocal consciousness, most people would say they've had experiences that can't be explained in any other way.

Another interesting study involving prayer was done at the Spindrift Foundation in Oregon. They split trays of plant seeds into sides A and B, and people at a distance prayed for either side. Time and again the prayed-for side did better. The question they asked was, What is the best type of prayer, directed or nondirected prayer? Directed prayer tells the universe what it's supposed to do—"I want X number of seeds to germinate," for example, or "I want the seeds to imbibe more water." Nondirected prayer says simply, "May the system manifest its best potential." It turned out that both kinds of prayer were effective, but nondirected prayer was two to four times as effective as directed prayer. This accords with ancient wisdom.

Don't push the river.

Yes. Any spiritual teacher will tell you not to pray that a person's difficult time be taken away, but to pray that the best in them manifest itself, that they have the strength and courage to make it through. This answers those who ask, If I'm trying to use imagery to heal something specific in my body, whether it's a wart or a tumor, should I specifically see the immune system running in and gobbling things up? Or should I send general healing energy to my body and ask for the blessing that the best will manifest?

You talked earlier about unhealthy guilt. There seems to be a tendency among people who get sick and are unable to cure themselves to feel guilty about it, as if they've failed in some way.

People will always prefer guilt over helplessness. No one wants to feel that they're completely powerless; they'd rather blame themselves, because in blame at least there's the sense that it's someone's fault. Why are bad things happening? We're still being punished for Eve's sin. If we're being punished, that means we're not powerless. If we follow certain moral precepts, we can be redeemed.

As I mentioned earlier, many people these days seem to be suffering from what Ken Wilber calls new age guilt. They feel that if they get cancer they must have eaten incorrectly or thought the wrong thing or not expressed their emotions properly. That gives them a greater feeling of power than if they say, "I really don't know why I got cancer." There is the sense that what you've created you can uncreate. Of course, for some kinds of cancers this may be true. As a cancer cell biologist, I can tell you that for some cancers in some people, a change in mental factors could change the course of the disease. But there are many other cancers that are biologically determined and couldn't be cured by even the best mental outlook and attitude.

I asked the Dalai Lama about this in India last fall. "There are people in this country," I said, "who, when they get ill, believe it must have been caused by their being psychologically or spiritually wrong in some way. What would you tell these people?" He had a great laugh. "I would tell them not to be so simple-minded," he said. "You have to look at genetics, at the environment, as well as at the effect of the mind on the body. When something bad happens in your life, it's always good to see how you might have contributed to it. But that doesn't mean you should blame yourself, because in some cases there will be a contribution and in others there won't."

So we need to have a healthy respect for the mystery of things, for the unknown.

Exactly. The Western mind doesn't respect the mystery. It believes that everything is knowable, that if, for example, we were to look hard enough at a particular case of cancer, we would be able to detect every factor that caused it.

In your book you talk not only about guilt, but also about shame. What's the difference between guilt and shame?

To begin with, there are two kinds of guilt: healthy guilt and unhealthy guilt. In healthy guilt, we realize that we did something hurtful to someone else and we feel bad about it. The healthy way to deal with healthy guilt is to take responsibility for what we did, make amends where possible, and then forgive ourselves and let go. If we can do that, healthy guilt teaches us compassion. But if we hold on to healthy guilt, it turns into an internalized source of shame, a feeling of basic unworthiness, that remains with us the rest of our lives.

Now there's another form of guilt that is always unhealthy and is intimately related to shame. Unhealthy guilt comes from the fear, based on the experiences of childhood, that we won't be good enough to get the love we so desperately desire. I consider this a kind of autoimmune disease of the soul, in which we attack our own substance as being unworthy. We all know people like this, who feel guilty and apologetic no matter how much they do for others. They can't take a compliment, because nothing they do is ever good enough in their eyes.

This set of responses, which I call unhealthy guilt—the inability to take compliments, the need for perfection, the self-deprecation—stems from what John Bradshaw calls toxic shame, shame at one's very identity. At the core of these responses is the fear that we're going to lose love because we're going to be judged unworthy—and the fear is so intense because love is primary to us as human beings. Babies who aren't touched don't put out growth hormones and eventually wither and die—what scientists call failure-to-thrive syndrome.

In human beings, it seems that the experience of not getting sufficient love as a child, if it doesn't turn into a failure-to-thrive syndrome and death, might in fact turn into shame, into an inherent sense of unworthiness, even if the child wasn't overtly shamed.

That's exactly right. And with that inherent sense of unworthiness, we're prone both to unhealthy guilt and to dealing with healthy guilt in an unhealthy way. When people with a shame-based identity do something wrong, they become so ashamed, so afraid that this really does mean they're worthless and that love will be withdrawn, that they have trouble taking responsibility for their actions and integrating their dark side. Such people develop huge shadows, a huge split between their good and bad sides, like the old story of Jekyll and Hyde. The nice side grows nicer while the shadow gets bigger and darker.

Robert Bly puts it well. He says that we arrive from the far reaches of the universe as 360-degree balls of radiance, place ourselves at our parents' feet, and say, "Here I am." And they say, "I didn't want you, I wanted a good little girl or boy." That's where the drama begins. All the parts of ourselves that are not affirmed or loved get tucked away in the shadow, which he calls a long bag we drag behind us. What we don't see composts in the bag, gets wild, builds up a big head of steam, while we expend all our energy maintaining a mask through which we purchase love and affection. At the same time, we project our dark side onto others. We don't see our own anger, we see the people around us as being angry. We don't see our own sadness, we find sad people to comfort. Unless we begin to heal that split, there's no way we can feel an authentic sense of happiness. When our identity is based on shame, when we have this tremendous fear that unless we're perfect in some way we're not going to be loved, our whole life becomes organized around the avoidance of fear rather than around the attraction of love. The question is, How can we heal this split?

This is the dimension that was missing in your earlier book. There you advised people to meditate and do yoga and perhaps even try psychotherapy, but you didn't address the healing of the split between the true and false selves.

Right. You can do therapy or meditation with the false self and never even touch the authentic self. This authentic self is the repository of all our creativity as well as our full range of emotions, the kinds of emotions that children express so freely, like joy and rage and hurt. When the true self is contacted, these emotions are expressed.

They're the carriers of our life energy. Without them, we don't have access to enough of our energy to heal the body-mind.

Exactly. If your energy is locked up in the shadow, your life force is low. Pessimistic people have lowered immune response and tend to have a range of illnesses that more optimistic people don't.

The question is, How do we heal this condition? Very often therapy is not enough. I'm reminded of Carl Jung's famous letter to Bill W., the founder of Alcoholics Anonymous. He told Bill that his drinking problem was too deep for just therapy, that it required a fundamental shift in belief systems toward something more spiritual. William James said the same thing in 1901, in his book *The Varieties of Religious Experience*. He was responding to the so-called New Thought movement, which was the new age of the late 19th century. James said that people could meditate or recite affirmations, but real change would only take place when they had encountered a deeper part within themselves, what we've been calling the true or authentic self. He saw this as a spiritual conversion, a recognition that we are innately good and that we live and move and have our being in a benign, loving consciousness.

Which is the kind of recognition that tends to accompany the experience of one's authentic self.

Yes. William James understood the problem of pessimism, which he called soul sickness, and the role of shame and guilt and the syndrome of the shame-based personality. The opposite, he said, is healthy-mindedness, and the way to get it is through a true spiritual conversion that affects the very depth of our being and restructures our psychological view of ourselves. And I don't think such a conversion is so hard for people to have.

Why?

The great Indian sage Sri Ramakrishna said, "The winds of grace are blowing all the time, you have only to raise your sail." Jesus said it differently: "Knock and the door will be opened." I see it all the time. We don't get help until we ask. But it's a hard lesson to learn for those of us with a shame-based identity. We don't want to ask for help because we're afraid we'll offend someone or be rejected. We have to learn to ask for help, both psychologically and spiritually. When we truly begin to open ourselves up with an appreciation of the power of nonlocal consciousness and simply say "May the means for my healing manifest themselves," I believe absolutely that help will be forthcoming. People who put out that message from the depths of their being are usually motivated to follow through and do something that quickens their inner life. Some meditate, some pray, some keep a dream journal, some simply set aside quiet time to invite a bit of sacred silence into their lives. As soon as we begin to open ourselves up, the universe rushes in.

Another thing to remember is that there's power in a group. Being with other people and telling your story can be very healing. In a Twelve Step program, for example, you realize that you're not the only sinner in the world, and you're not the only one who experiences such terrible guilt and shame. In my experience, people with problems of shame or abuse in childhood who join a Twelve Step program seem to undergo greater healing than those who just do psychotherapy.

People who belong to meditation or prayer groups report that when they're meditating or praying for someone else, the healing they feel within themselves is remarkable. There's a tremendous sense of love that opens the heart, and suddenly no one has to tell them they're worthy, they know it because they feel it as a flow of love deep inside. Until we feel this flow of love within, we can do all the psychotherapy in the world, and it will just be words.

Earlier you mentioned the role of forgiveness. How does that relate to surrendering or opening ourselves to the winds of grace?

Forgiveness is more than a function, more than something we do or say to others (or to ourselves) after they (or we) have done something wrong. Forgiveness is an attitude of nonjudgmentalness, whereby we're always looking for the true self in another person, the spark of divinity, the best, the creative potential. If somebody does something you really don't like and you're relating to them from the self in you rather than from some unhealed or shadow part, you can be authentic with them and say, "What you did made me angry, you overstepped my bounds," while still continuing to see the best in them.

Let me tell you a story about my second book, *Guilt Is the Teacher, Love Is the Lesson.* I was writing about the importance of forgiveness in relating to guilt. In unhealthy guilt, we have to forgive ourselves in order to heal the sense of shame that feeds it. In healthy guilt, we need to perform a set of actions based on forgiveness in order to deal with the guilt in a healthy way: we have to take responsibility, make appropriate restitution, communicate about what we have done, learn what we can from it, and then let it go.

As I was typing the words "healthy guilt" onto my word processor, it switched for no apparent reason into bold italics—an operation that would ordinarily have taken several separate steps. Not only that, it split the phrase into three words: "heal thy guilt." I had to get up from the computer and sit for a while to contemplate what that meant in my own life. Of course, that's the heart of forgiveness—the process of coming to forgiveness within ourselves, which means a new sense of who we really are. Plus it's an attitude of trying to relate true self to true self. As the Indians say, "Namaste"—the divinity in me recognizes and salutes the divinity in you. Plus forgiveness is also a set of actions necessary to transmute healthy guilt into wisdom. It's all three. I had to put that chapter down and come back to it months later after I had done some work on myself.

Jacob Needleman

It's a gray winter day in San Francisco's Sunset District, and I'm driving along deserted, treeless streets looking for a corner storefront where I'm to meet philosopher Jacob Needleman. The locals are apparently gone for the day, and I feel strangely adrift and alone, as if I were wandering the landscape of another planet, destination unknown, hoping to connect with some other life forms.

At last I find what I've been looking for, the street number painted the same color as the wall and barely visible, the windows covered with drapes from top to bottom, no sign of life or light inside. I knock hesitantly, thinking perhaps I'm mistaken after all—wrong day, wrong address, wrong person—but Jerry Needleman (as he likes to be called) comes to the door immediately and ushers me in.

I'm surprised by what I encounter. Expecting a bustling office with computers and bulletin boards and other accoutrements of the busy professor, I'm delighted to find a spacious, nearly empty room unlighted except for a soft glow from the street. This is Needleman's home away from home, a space he rents for workshops and seminars, a place where he can take refuge when the demands of home and work require it.

Needleman, too, is a pleasant surprise. Where I had expected to meet a gruff, hard-bitten intellectual, I find instead an exceedingly gentle, accessible man with none of the rigidity or formality one associates with academia. He is short, round, graying, with expressive eyes capable of moving quickly from thoughtfulness to delight. As we sound one another out with the usual pre-interview chitchat, I feel unaccountably at ease with this man, as if we've known one another for a long time—indeed, as if, instead of eminent professor and journalist, we're colleagues in some vast project of collective awakening.

The author of over half a dozen books on consciousness and spirituality and editor of the Penguin Metaphysical Library, Needleman is probably best known for *The New Religions* (1970), a pioneering exploration of this country's emerging love affair with Eastern philosophy. Yet the principal focus of much of his work has been not to describe preestablished truths, but to challenge his readers to ask the great existential questions for themselves: Who am I? Why am I here? What is the meaning and purpose of life? Following the lead of Socrates, who said, "The unexamined life is not worth living," Needleman refuses to accept dogma at face value. Instead, in book after book, he is constantly pushing us (again like his Greek counterpart) to probe further and question more deeply.

Reading in Needleman's writings over the years, I have been particularly impressed by his sage observations on the spiritual path and by his insights into the connection between personal growth and spiritual transformation. I decided to contact him when I saw that he would be offering a workshop exploring spiritual perspectives on loneliness. "Fascinating," I thought. "I wonder what he's come up with this time." For Needleman has been thinking about these issues far longer than the rest of us, with the rigor and intensity of a true philosopher.

Born and raised in Philadelphia, Needleman went to Harvard with the intention of preparing for medical school. Like so many others of his generation, who came of age in the '50s, however, he was soon hooked on existentialism, and decided to major in philosophy. Troubled by the "gut-level" questions he now asks of his students, Needleman met with uncomprehending stares from his professors, for whom existentialism was largely an aberration from the philosophical mainstream.

"The implication," he says, "was that I needed a psychiatrist, not a philosopher. Fortunately, visitors came through Harvard from time to time who had another vision of the greatness of the philosophical tradition."

One such visitor was Rasvihari Das, one of India's most eminent philosophers, with whom Needleman formed a kind of guru-disciple relationship. "I was the only one who signed up for his course on Vedanta," he recalls. "He worked my brain very hard, and my heart too."

After completing his doctorate at Yale, where he became interested in

Zen and the "whole question of inner development," Needleman accepted a teaching position at San Francisco State University. When asked to give a course in Western religious thought, he agreed grudgingly, but soon developed a fascination with both the Western and Eastern spiritual traditions. In addition to his abiding interest in Zen, he has for many years been immersed in the teachings of G. I. Gurdjieff.

Needleman still teaches philosophy at San Francisco State (his classes are immensely popular), as well as offering workshops and seminars designed to bring the perennial philosophy to a broad audience, from businesspeople to health professionals. His most recent book, *Money and the Meaning of Life*, explores "the role of money in the search for consciousness," and he has shared his ideas with Bill Moyers on the PBS show *A World of Ideas*.

In addition to his other projects, Needleman has helped establish an audiocassette series entitled Audio Literature, in which he and other luminaries read great spiritual classics like the *Bhagavad Gita*, the *Tao Te Ching*, Shunryu Suzuki's *Zen Mind, Beginner's Mind*, and *The Cloud of Unknowing*. Most of these texts were meant to be read aloud, Needleman contends, so they could enter into an entirely different dimension of our being.

Before we begin our interview, we listen for a few moments to Robert Bly reading poems by the Sufi poet Kabir. As Bly's voice rises and falls hypnotically to a sitar accompaniment, I find myself lulled into a relaxed, receptive state. This, I think to myself, is philosophy as it was meant to be experienced—not with the head only, but with the heart as well.

Jacob Needleman

The Heart of Philsopby

When we think of philosophy in the West, we generally think of ivy-covered walls and dry expositions about the nature of reality. We don't ordinarily associate philosophy with the heart. One of your recent books is entitled The Heart of Philosophy, *so clearly you have a very different view on the matter. One of the things you are trying to awaken in people, it seems, is an appreciation of the true meaning or purpose of philosophy.*

Yes, philosophy is really a form of being in love. It's a love or striving for wisdom—wisdom not as knowledge, but as a state of being, a state of consciousness, a state of inner transformation and understanding. The true philosopher of ancient times strove for such wisdom. Plato called this striving *eros*, the love for being, for meaning, for participation in what is ultimately real and meaningful. In our modern culture, we have confined the word *eros* to the sexual side of life. Plato did not ignore this side, but he said that there is another force in the human psyche, which modern psychology has not really recognized. This yearning or striving for transcendence, for being, is probably the most important part of the psyche—but it has been ignored.

Freud, for example, reduces it to sublimated sexuality.

Yes. Freud was a great pioneer in certain areas, and I admire what he did, but in this area I would say he was uninformed. Now modern philosophy in the West has not kept up with that personal, interior passion for meaning and being, understanding and inner self-development. Philosophy is basically a spiritual quest, and it makes use of the mind in a way that some other strategies don't. If you like, you could say it's a step toward a Western jnana [wisdom] yoga. Or at least it's a pathway toward the path, if not a path itself in the sense of a discipline of self-development. It's very important to have this in our culture.

Philosophy, then, leads the mind toward inquiry, toward asking the right questions that will ultimately lead one onto the spiritual path?

Yes, but mainstream philosophy today has modeled the search for wisdom after the kinds of thinking and standards of knowing that modern science uses, which is a tremendous mistake. Science is very good in certain areas of inquiry, but completely helpless in many ways when it comes to searching for wisdom. All the spiritual traditions have recognized this force within us, this striving, though they have given it different names. In the Buddhist tradition there is a wonderful passage in one of the scriptures describing a day in the life of the Buddha. Before the Buddha goes to bed, it says, he "casts his Buddha eye around the world to see who has the Great Wish" and draws that person to him. It's this "Great Wish" that philosophy is about. But it has almost totally disappeared from the academic field. In that sense I'm very much outside the philosophical mainstream, although there is a growing movement back to find the real heart of philosophy.

Socrates, who I understand is a favorite of yours, said, "Learning is remembering." And in your books you use the term "remembering" in a certain way. What exactly do you (and Socrates) mean by this term?

The German word for remembering literally means "to go inside." To remember is to go inside. There is something within each of us that needs to be contacted, a great force or understanding that needs to be developed. Philosophy, as remembering, is the art or discipline of opening to that inner understanding. The teachings of all the great traditions say the same thing. We have "it" within us, but we are alienated from it. And there is a kind of mind in us that is meant to act as a servant or instrument of something higher. Our ordinary cerebral intellect is more like a computer, but it has been mistaken for the real mind. Plato and Socrates try to bring the intellect to a grinding halt, so that it will move out of the way and allow us to return to the other mind. Philosophy is meant to assist in that process. That's why he calls it remembering.

So Socrates and Plato "do" philosophy instead of just writing about it. That is, they pursue philosophy as an activity as opposed to an exercise of the intellect.

Yes, they do it, they live it. Socrates was a real master.

The process you describe sounds like working with a Zen koan: stopping the mind and forcing it to go inward so it can, as you say, remember what it already knows.

Yes. This is also what I attempt to do in my philosophy classes, while at the same time trying to maintain academic form and respectability and do the work that has to be done. I'm trying to give students a taste of this other thing which cannot be taught in a university setting. Teaching philosophy, for me, is a very necessary response to the spiritual hunger of people today. People are starving for something, and not everyone feels comfortable turning to a foreign or alien culture to get it. When they can find it in their own culture, at the heart of philosophy or Christianity or Judaism, something really comes alive in them. Working in that way with people is very rewarding for me. In all of my classes and workshops, I try to create the conditions in which something can really pass between people, something that's not presently passing but is meant to pass. Something finer is not being transferred; people are starving and they don't know why. I try to create a relationship with people based on this mutual inquiry and search, which is what Plato called real friendship.

Can you say a little more about this "something" that is supposed to pass between people but isn't?

It's a kind of energy or force—I don't really know what to call it. But it's something we feed each other with. People, like all creatures, are nourished by something that's not tangible. Call it a vibration or emanation, if you like. People give it to each other, plants give it to people, and all of nature is related, not just through the more obvious forms of food, but through other kinds of energies in the universe. So people need something from each other that goes beyond words or sex or physical contact. You might call it attention. When I give real attention to you, or you to me, when I really listen to you, or you listen to me, it's not just that I'm flattered. Something is passing—something that needs to pass.

Wouldn't "love" be a good name for it?

Absolutely. Why not? Of course, one feels this something very strongly in the presence of a truly great master. But even among people like you and me, something can pass between us that is needed. It comes through opening, listening, giving one's attention. People are starved for this. Many of the ancient rituals and forms of relationship, which we think of as being cumbersome and uncomfortable, had that as their main purpose. This is also the real force at work in healing and in psychotherapy, although I don't know if all therapists understand it. Freud was probably a good therapist because he gave people attention in a way that nobody had given it before.

Yes. So many people come into therapy suffering from a lack of being heard, received, appreciated—by their loved ones, their parents, themselves. What the therapist does that is most healing, often, is to give them that loving, non-judgmental, non-demanding attention.

Yes.

I also think that one of the reasons people are constantly trying to fall in love is that, at least at the beginning of a love relationship, they receive that kind of rapt attention. Then the attention starts fading and the person feels disgruntled and leaves. Really, that's what we're all looking for.

I think so. Psychotherapists have such a huge job to do. People are so lonely, so unhappy, so frightened, so bewildered and tense. We all are. It's a critical time.

Say more about the loneliness.

Several years ago I asked one of my classes, "What do you consider to be the major problems of our society?" I got the usual answers: the breakdown of the family, nuclear war, ecology. Then somebody said "loneliness." So I asked, "How many people here feel basically lonely?" Everyone raised their hand. I was astonished. Then I asked another, larger class, which had a much broader spectrum of people, and all but two people raised their hands. So I became very interested in loneliness. Then a 35-year-old black student from Nigeria said, "You know, when I first came from Nigeria to England, I didn't understand what people meant when they said they were lonely. It's only now, after I've been living in the United States for two years, that I know what it means to be lonely." In his culture, loneliness simply didn't exist; they didn't even have a word for it. There was plenty of pain, plenty of suffering, plenty of grief, but no loneliness.So what is this loneliness we're experiencing? People are cut off, not just from each other, but also from some harmonizing force in themselves. It's not just that "I am lonely"; it's that the "I" is lonely. We are lacking an essential harmonious relationship with some universal force. To me, this is why loneliness is an important phenomenon to understand.

It's similar to what we were talking about before—our lack of connectedness and our failure to get nourishment from others or from ourselves.

Right. Loneliness has been looked at psychologically and sociologically, but not spiritually and metaphysically.

When I think about loneliness, I generally think that in our culture we no longer have the opportunity to see ourselves as part of a fabric or network or closely interconnected web of being. We see ourselves rather as individuals cut off from the whole. Family ties, even friendships, no longer have the strength to hold people together.

That's right. I think this is an important moment in history. When I spoke with Krishnamurti shortly before his death, I said to him, "Would you say things are worse now than when you started, or better?" And he said, "Worse." I said, "I have the feeling that we are at a real moment of crisis." And he said, "It's very true, this is a very critical period right now."

Say a little more about this "critical period."

I think it's connected to what I said before about something not passing between people. Why is man on Earth? Everybody who is serious thinks about that question in some way. We recognize it but can't answer it. We know from the study of ecology that animals don't exist just to have fun. Everything has a purpose, a function, and something material to contribute to the pulsing movement of life. Every thing, every species is here for a reason. Similarly, everything in the human organism is there for a purpose. The heart, the tissues, the cells, the bone—everything is giving out something, paying something, delivering some energy or substance, as well as receiving something in return. So we begin to ask, What is man here for? Are we here just to think? No, there must be something we have to produce, something we have to deliver in material form. It's a finer substance, if you like, or a finer energy. Our purpose is to be the "nerve ends of the Earth," or something like that. And if we're not going to fulfill our purpose, the Earth itself may be in danger. This is the crisis we find ourselves in at this moment.

So we're not fulfilling our function?

Right. We're not fulfilling our cosmic duty—which we can only fulfill through an inner development that the ancient traditions have always spoken about. I think if we don't do that, then there may be massive changes in human life on Earth. It's that clear a crisis. And I don't know how much time we have left.

Then it's not fundamentally a political or ecological crisis?

No. The political and ecological crises are effects of the spiritual crisis. We're not conducting our lives properly, and our inner life doesn't proceed the way it was meant to. The issue is survival in the deepest sense of that term.

In the Sufi tradition, and also in the mystical Jewish tradition, there is the sense that man was created in order to love God. What you are saying sounds similar.

It is. But if taken superficially, the phrase "in order to love God" makes it sound as though we have a vain God who just needs creatures to make him feel good. We have to penetrate that expression more deeply. What does it really mean to "love God?" Does it mean to love God like you love ice cream or a work of art or another person? I think it must mean, at the very least, that you are guided by a very deep wish or force that puts first something that is not usually put first. It means to wish from deep within yourself to serve a higher purpose. How do you serve that purpose? It may mean that you allow something to elaborate in your very body that otherwise would not. You could call it making a passage from a higher realm down to the Earth, and vice versa. In the spiritual traditions this is symbolized by incarnation. For Christians, the incarnation is Jesus; other traditions refer to the avatar, the Buddha, and so forth. It's the idea that "as it is in heaven, so shall it be on Earth."

This is not just a metaphor; something has to come down onto the Earth. Man is like the bridge between heaven and Earth, over which this "something" has to pass. This is an old mystical idea found in Buddhism, in Christianity, in Judaism. It's the idea that the human being is central and exists at the key juncture of the cosmic scheme so that something can pass through him. If what needs to pass through him doesn't pass through, that which is below man will starve, and that branch of the tree of creation may wither. In other words, that which depends on man may perish, and nature in its greatness may find another route to get what it needs. In the Judaic tradition there are legends of God creating many, many experiments and wiping them out or letting them self-destruct because they didn't conform to their intended purpose. We may be just the most recent experiment.

It's a humbling thought.

Yes. At the same time, if you study the great spiritual teachings carefully, you realize that there is nothing hostile in this idea. There's a great mercy awaiting us; all we need to do is turn. Once we turn, all is going to be given to us. But unless we turn, it's like keeping our mouth shut so food can't enter. You can lead a horse to water but, as a great master once put it, you can't make him thirsty. We have to become thirsty. We have to attune ourselves in order to bring down that energy. That's what spiritual practice is about—attuning ourselves in that way.

You have written quite a bit about the relationship between psychotherapy and spiritual practice. In one book you suggest that psychotherapy is about the animal man—our incarnation—whereas spiritual practice is about transcending, going beyond. How do you see them as working together or being different? Another view might be that therapists are the new priests or ministers of our age.

To make broad generalizations, I think that therapists, when they're honest, don't presume to be leading people toward spiritual transcendence. On the whole, people go to therapists because they're not functioning well. They're frightened, they're angry, they lack self-esteem, and they're suffering in a way that makes it difficult for them to stand on their own two feet. Therapy can help people get back on their own feet and function in a relatively normal way. It's a means to an end. One doesn't think of therapy as a life-long commitment. You go with a problem you want to solve.

At the same time, something deeper can be opened with certain kinds of therapy. But a therapist has to recognize the difference between a psychological problem and a spiritual question. A spiritual question is not a sign of illness; it's a sign of health. And it's not necessary for a spiritual question to be "solved" or "fixed." In fact, it needs to be deepened—so much so that it becomes a force, like eros. But a psychological problem is something that needs to be repaired in some way. I think those are two different aims. And a therapist needs to recognize this, because what presents itself as a psychological problem may actually be a spiritual problem. A good therapist can see that the person is in the wrong place for the kind of problem she has.

The danger is that a therapist who doesn't know about the spiritual dimension can be so successful, as it were, at curing the psychological problem that he stamps out this very fragile spiritual question. Some of our suffering is inherent in the human condition; some of it is the result of our own hang-ups. Nobody's going to cure me of the human condition; certainly no therapist as such. But she may be able to cure my hang-up so well that I walk out feeling that everything's just great—to such an extent that I lose that fragile question.

Freud had a handle on this when he said we have to trade our neurotic suffering for ordinary, everyday human suffering.

Yes, that's the way I would put it. These days, things have gotten more complicated. Transpersonal psychologists are taking techniques from the spiritual traditions and using them for therapeutic purposes. Of course, therapy can be the first step toward spiritual development. But the therapist can be your guru only up to a point. Sometimes one prepares for the other. Sometimes they're absolutely opposite. It's a question of discernment, as in everything else.

In our society these days, personal growth and spiritual growth are lumped together. People talk of "personal and spiritual growth," as if they were synonymous. The question, it seems to me, is, What grows? Personal growth seems to be very different from spiritual growth. In fact, what looks like spiritual growth may be just an inflation of the ego—what Chogyam Trungpa calls spiritual materialism.

Yes. In personal growth we grow in wisdom and experience and tolerance, as well as emotional stability. But that's normal growth — it's not the same thing as spiritual growth. Spiritual growth involves transformation. It's one thing to have a car and want to make it a good car, but it's quite another thing to want to make it an airplane. Spirituality turns the car into an airplane. Psychotherapy helps to make the car run well.

It's not always such a clear-cut distinction, though, is it? I think, for example, of loneliness. If you feel lonely, is that a personal issue or a spiritual issue? Do you go to a therapist or to a spiritual teacher? It's really hard to know. What about fear, anger, or other strong emotions? There are certain teachings within the spiritual traditions—for example, in Tibetan Buddhism—about dealing with the emotions, which are certainly very wonderful ways of transcending and working with them. Does one want to go that way? Or does one want to try primal therapy or Gestalt or bioenergetics? How to know? We all have spiritual aspirations at some level or another. But exactly which set of remedies does one take for one's particular spiritual ills?

We can't know. We can have a hunch, but it's up to the teacher to know. The teacher needs to be insightful enough to be able to create conditions where people can find out for themselves if what they want is life-long service to higher inner development or relief from a painful psychological problem.

Brother David Steindl-Rast

Brother David Steindl-Rast is often considered Thomas Merton's successor as a builder of bridges between the Christian contemplative tradition and the meditative traditions of the East.

Born in Vienna in 1926 and raised a Catholic, Steindl-Rast witnessed, as a young man in postwar Austria, a flowering of interest in Eastern ways that was every bit as intense as America's in the 1970s. But "I was already rooted in one tradition," he explains, "which I found quite nourishing. I was mildly interested in what was going on, but I never read much about it."

In university he studied art, art history, anthropology, and psychology and graduated in 1952 with a doctorate in psychology from the University of Vienna. In 1953 he emigrated to the United States with vague visions of material success. "I had no intention of becoming a monk," he insists. However, after reading *The Rule of St. Benedict* (a classic guide to the monastic life), he visited Mount Savior Benedictine Monastery in upstate New York and knew within hours that he would stay. He has been a monk of Mount Savior ever since.

In the 1960s Steindl-Rast began encountering monks of other religious persuasions, including Buddhists and Hindus, and this prompted him to question whether "these were monks in the same sense in which we were monks." His reading in the monastic literature of Asia surprised him because "some of the details of the training were so similar to our own—unaccountably so, because there was no external influence of one on the other."

In 1965 Steindl-Rast met the Buddhist monk Eido Tai Shimano of the Zen Studies Society of New York. "When we met, it was clear to both of us that despite all the cultural differences, we really spoke one language. Eido Roshi invited me to spend some time with him in New York."

With the permission of his prior—"a very forward-looking, open-minded man"—Steindl-Rast went on to spend a total of three years in residence at the Zen center in New York, practicing meditation and studying with such prominent masters as Soen Nakagawa and Hakuun Yasutani. He also spent a summer and a training period at Tassajara Zen Mountain Center with Shunryu Suzuki Roshi, author of *Zen Mind, Beginner's Mind.*

"I can still remember the first time I went to Tassajara," Steindl-Rast recalls. "I had been visiting a Trappist monastery the week before, and when I got to Tassajara I became confused as to whether I was now in a Christian monastery or a Buddhist monastery. They looked the same, the schedule was practically the same, the inner attitude—everything was the same. And it worked both ways. Ten minutes after I came, everybody took to me as if I had always been there."

Also at about this time, Steindl-Rast's prior took him to see Merton. "Merton was very interested in my practical exposure and experience, and I was very interested in his theoretical knowledge. He was never really exposed to the practice himself until he traveled to India, where he met a number of different teachers. His initial contact was entirely intellectual, whereas mine was primarily through practice."

Steindl-Rast's outreach has not been limited to the East-West ecumenical dialogue, however. During the several months each year when he is not in hermitage, he travels and teaches throughout the world, "trying," as he puts it, "to address myself to the great issues of our time"—among them world hunger and the threat of nuclear destruction—"which always have a spiritual side. . . . One of my great concerns is how we can get the message of peace to as many people as possible."

In recent years Steindl-Rast has drastically reduced his lecturing to devote more time to what he calls his "avocation": the hermit's life. Still dedicated to his original monastic community of Mount Savior, he has established as home base the Immaculate Heart Hermitage in Big Sur, California, because, in his words, "the Camaldolese pattern of the community here holds great promise for the future of monastic life. In contrast to most other monks, whose one focus is community, Camaldolese monks swing back and forth between three equally important focal points: hermit's life, outreach in service beyond the monastery, and, between these two, life in monastic community."

In addition to his previous works, *A Listening Heart* and *Gratefulness, the Heart of Prayer*, Steindl-Rast has coauthored a book with Fritjof Capra entitled *New Thinking on God and Nature* and is at work on another with American Zen teacher Robert Aitken. Recently he had the "privilege" of cofounding the first Buddhist-Christian center in his native Austria, and he has been a regular faculty member at the annual Christian-Buddhist meditation symposium at Naropa Institute in Colorado.

When I meet with Brother David at the San Francisco Zen Center, where he is a frequent guest, I'm surprised to find so much genuine humility in a man of such stature. Soft-spoken and slight of build, with deep-set, compassionate eyes, he seems constantly attentive ("listening," as he puts it) to the call of the present moment—a virtue cultivated during long years of contemplation. Yet his gentleness is tempered by an air of authority and conviction and a fullness of presence that customarily accompany a rich inner life.

This unique combination of qualities—gentleness and strength, humility and fervor—remind me of accomplished Buddhist monks I have known. Indeed, with firm roots in his own tradition and intensive training in Eastern practices, Steindl-Rast himself embodies the bridging of East and West that he has so eloquently espoused.

David Steindl-Rast

Seeking the Heart of Prayer

Tell me, Brother David, now that you've had the opportunity to explore the Eastern traditions, particularly Buddhism, what do you think Buddhism has to offer Christianity, particularly Catholicism?

Let me approach this question on several levels. On one level, I think religious traditions go through phases, through ups and downs, and Buddhism in this country right now is going through a very fervent phase. When you go to most Zen centers here, you find not so much a focus on theories or doctrines as a strong emphasis on practice.

Unfortunately, in Catholic monasteries right now we don't have that fervor of practice. Maybe it's not so much a matter of inner attitude as a matter of not really knowing what to do. In most monasteries there are a few people who practice Zen or yoga because it is how they can express their fervor. They feel, rightly or wrongly—and I think largely wrongly—that they cannot find similarly effective methods in our Christian monastic tradition.

So that is one area in which we can learn from Eastern ways. We can take over some methods that are universally applicable, such as Zen sitting, or hatha yoga, or pranayama.

But then, on a deeper level, there is a complementarity, in the Christian and Buddhists approaches, between word and silence. The whole Western religious tradition in centered on the word. Perhaps the key intuition of the biblical religions is that "God speaks." Therefore, everything that *is*, is "word," mythologically expressed by the fact that God spoke, and there it was. God said, "Let there be light," and there was light; God said, "Let there be animals," and there were all the animals; and so forth.

Then humans began, by speaking, to appropriate the word. Adam gives names to everything; he gives names to the animals and so has a handle on them. The key practice, the key virtue in this tradition, is trust and obedience to the spoken word. One listens lovingly, one opens one's ears and responds to the word. This is a wonderful realm of spirituality belonging to all human beings; everybody can understand it on some level.

But when you focus so much on the word, you tend to neglect the realm of silence. That is the complementarity that Buddhism brings, because Buddhism is all about silence. Buddhism teaches us to throw ourselves forever and ever into that silence, and that in turn creates the horizon from which the word can be understood and seen. This is what Merton meant, I'm sure, when he said that he could not have understood the Christian tradition as he did except from the Buddhist perspective. This silence creates the background against which you can see the word.

Then, of course, there is a third dimension, the dimension of action, of understanding. In the Eastern traditions you understand by acting, you don't understand by sitting back. To understand swimming, you have to jump into the water. I remember Swami Venkatesananda saying, "Yoga *is* understanding." In all the different branches of yoga, you do something, and in the doing you understand it from within. So we as Christians say, "Yes, our specialty is the word, but there is no word without silence, and there is no word or silence without understanding and doing." This forms a kind of trinitarian approach. Jesus is the Word, the Father is the silence out of which the Word comes, and the Holy Spirit is that spirit of understanding in which we act and labor and move and have our being. I've found this to be an approach that is not threatening to others and yet does justice to the Christian tradition.

What, on the other hand, do you feel Christianity might have to offer to Buddhism and Hinduism that might enrich those traditions?

I'm somewhat reluctant to blow my own horn, so to speak. But what I have heard Buddhists, even the Dalai Lama, say over and over again is that, at this present juncture in history, social consciousness, service, and compassionate action have been organized and developed more extensively by Christians. That would be one area in which we could find common ground and work together. Then of course there's the making explicit. If the "religions of the book" have the word as their specialty, it stands to reason that they would be able to speak most articulately about what's happening to all of us as a human family. Therefore, articulate books can be written about Buddhism and Hinduism by Christians.

Brother David, I've heard it said, "Since all paths lead to the same place anyway, choose the path that has heart for you." Do you agree that all paths lead to the same place?

It depends on what you mean by "paths." We tend to speak about where a path leads, but it helps to ask where a path starts. If it is a path with heart, it starts in the heart, in the human heart. I have never met any human being in all my travels—and I have traveled extensively, including time spent with Native American peoples, with Australian Aborigines, and with the Maoris in New Zealand—that gave me the slightest doubt that in our heart of hearts we are all one. Not just similar—one; there is only one human heart.

And that is where the path starts. It starts when we discover, in some way or other, that deep sense of belonging. You could call it all-oneness or cosmic unity; my favorite word for it is "belonging." Most of us as children already have a lively sense of it. As adults we experience it sometimes in nature, or with other human beings. And this deep sense of belonging could actually be called "home." Home is where we start from, as T. S. Eliot says. "And the end of all our exploring will be to arrive where we started and know the place for the first time." So the end-point of the path is to get home again. This longing for belonging, this homing instinct of the heart, is the path within every path.

But when you ask if all paths lead to the same place, and then think of the manifestations of that longing, you have to be very careful. In all the traditions I am familiar with, the inner path leads to the same goal. But sometimes the outer path can distract you from this inner path. In the Christian tradition this one universal path with heart is to be found all the different denominations. But every denomination, my own certainly not excluded, also has aspects that would be detrimental to your ever reaching your goal. So I take a very cautious view of religions, including my own, because they have a built-in tendency to become irreligious. Our task, if we belong to a religion, is to make our particular religion religious, to transform it into the "path with heart." You can sit zazen or do all the things Catholics are supposed to do, and it won't get you anywhere, unless you do it with heart, unless you find that center were you're really at home. And then you're already there.

Studying other traditions can perhaps help revive in us a sense of that heart we're starting from.

Very much so, both in a negative way and in a positive way. After we've seen all the shortcomings of other religions, we can turn around and more easily see the shortcomings in our own. That's the negative approach. But if you're open-minded, you can also see in every tradition people who are dedicated and alive, great teachers who are very inspiring, and all of a sudden you have a much fuller calendar of saints than you had before. On All Saints Day, for instance, in our petitions in the monastery, all the great teachers from the Buddhist and Hindu traditions are being mentioned nowadays without anybody batting an eyelash. In fact, we've had the Buddha in our calendar since the sixth century, when John of Damascus picked up his story from monks wandering from Asia Minor. He's called St. Jehosephat, which is a transliteration of the Sanskrit *bodhisattva*, "enlightened being."

You've written, "The closer you come to the heart of your own tradition, the closer you come to the heart of other traditions." I wonder how you feel about young people who are brought up in the Christian tradition who then leave it to look elsewhere for guidance, for a path they can call their own. Do you feel that this is appropriate and that they will ultimately find what they're looking for? Or do you feel that at some point they will have to come back and resolve their relationship with their own tradition?

The one thing we will always have to find, of course, is our own center; not some teaching out there, but our own innermost heart. If the tradition in which you were brought up hasn't helped you find that, then I feel very good about your looking for it somewhere else because I have hopes that your search will be successful.

But I also feel sad when I look at how much my own religion has given me, and how much it could give to other people, and I realize that something seems to be lacking there, in the educational institutions or in the family. I can't quite put my finger on it. So young people frequently have to leave and go browsing, and this makes me sad. But I am happy when I see that these young people at least have guts and interest and religious spunk enough to look for it somewhere else.

As for the child who has gone through Catholic schools and has had Catholic parents and whose parents are not distressed because he or she all of a sudden puts on Buddhist robes or goes to India or whatever, my only concern at this point is for the parents. I always try to tell them, "Rejoice with your child, because this child, has, under a different cover, under a different label, found what is so important to *you*." I try to broaden their minds a little. I have no doubt at all that these young people, if they continue on the path they have chosen, will find what we call "Christ." Because I know you can find it in all the different traditions. Very frequently, of course, it happens that people who come from a Christian background spend many years practicing Zen, for instance, or yoga, and eventually, through this practice—not in spite of it, but through it—rediscover their Christian background.

But by this I don't mean to imply that I'm a nominalist. I don't say "It's all the same." The paths are very, very different. The more you study them, the more you realize that they are far more different than we had originally thought. On the surface there is a certain similarity, and deep down there is a oneness. But between those two poles they are as different as they can possibly be. And that's good, because there is something for everybody.

Religions are like human beings, it seems. On the surface we're very much the same—we have two eyes, a nose, a mouth—and deep down we have the same heart. But our personalities are quite different.

That's exactly the parallel. Therefore different human beings have to follow different paths to find that oneness which we really all have—with other human beings, with animals, with plants, with the whole cosmos. To arrive there is bliss, the path of heart.

The word "contemplative" is often used to describe monks in the Benedictine order, the order of which you're a part. What is contemplation, as you practice it, and how does it differ from meditation, in the Eastern sense? I'm particularly interested in the word "contemplation" and how that differs from "meditation."

In literature you will find the words "meditation" and "contemplation" used in different ways. In the Christian tradition, meditation emphasizes more *your* doing; you take a passage and you meditation it, which means that you think about it on a deeper level, perhaps, or you move it lovingly around in your heart, or you repeat the mantra, or whatever. Then comes a higher stage called "contemplation," where you are no longer in control of the process. Instead, you open yourself, you drop the word or passage or the image you've been dealing with, and you're just *there*. And this does something to you. Not when we speak more broadly of monastic life as the "contemplative life," we mean a life-style in which people give priority to meditation and contemplation, to prayer, to spiritual practices. These are roughly the definitions most people would agree to in everyday parlance.

To do justice to your excellent question, however, one would have to go much deeper and ask what the term *contemplatio* originally meant. This Latin term expresses one of the most primordial religious attitudes we can trace, an attitude based on the idea that the higher things set the pattern for order in the lower things. The *templum*, which we now call "temple," was originally not a building but a measured-out area in the sky, and the sky, with all its planets and stars, was the symbol for cosmic order. The Roman priests and augurs consulted the heavens, the temple, took the order they found there, and projected it onto the chaos of daily living.

In my opinion, this idea of contemplation is really the predominant one. It implies that every human being has a contemplative tendency, a contemplative life, which is that aspect of your inner life by which you seek meaning. Corresponding to the higher things would be meaning; corresponding to the lower things would be daily life, purpose, purposeful action. To put meaning into your purpose—that is how I understand "contemplation;" to raise up your eyes and look at that which gives meaning to your life, at the higher, unchangeable things, and to try to put your life in order.

From this perspective you can understand that monastic life is not called contemplative simply because monks have a little more time to meditate or pray. The real reason is that monks in all the different monastic traditions—being extremely sensitive to the chaos in the world—step back a little and say, "Let's build now within this chaotic world a little island of order." That is the monastery—not the buildings, particularly, but a place where time and space are put in order. Schedules are marked by gongs and bells and clappers and drums. Certain things are done in certain places and not in others; you take off your shoes and put them in a certain place; you dress in a certain way; and so forth.

This external way of ordering time and space is very important to monastic life, but all the achieved monks will tell you that it is really not of ultimate importance. The decisive thing is that you put your life in order; *that* is contemplative life. The monastery is like a controlled environment or laboratory for this particular pursuit. St. Benedict calls it a "workshop for the divine life."

What about the relationship between contemplation and social action? Most people think that the one precludes the other, whereas I sense that you have combined them in your life.

Given the understanding of contemplation that I just shared with you, it becomes obvious that the two belong together, because where do you draw the line in transforming the world?

So both social action and contemplation attempt to put the world in order.

That's right, attempt to bring order into life. The monastery draws a line and erects a fence, but only in order to set up a model or a focal point or a workshop whose influence radiates out.

In practice, however, it isn't that easy. For one thing, the pursuits are obviously quite different, more now than in former times. In the Middle Ages you could run a school or hospital right in the middle of the monastery itself. Nowadays, a school or hospital has become something so totally different in its demands from a monastery that it is almost impossible to hold these two dimensions together. Life has become highly specialized, the demands are quite divergent, and our energies are limited. You might well think, "Life is too short to become a really good monk who stays in the monastery all the time." And that is true. But since life also demands both activities from me, I find myself trying to respond to the demands of life, and I end up not doing either one so very well. I have great compassion for others who make different choices, because I see how difficult it is for me. Right now, in fact, I'm cutting down on the time I spend traveling, saying no to three out of four invitations to speak, just because I feel it is more and more important for me to stay in the monastery. I need to weigh whether I can do more, at this point, by writing than by going out and meeting a relatively small group of people.

So the two are compatible in your eyes; in fact, contemplation seems to imply social action. Yet our time and energy are limited.

They're not just compatible; they are two aspects of the same reality. But to put the two together is very difficult. One solution is to go back and forth between these two poles. Sometimes you totally immerse yourself in the vision, to the exclusion of all action, as far as possible. At other times you totally immerse yourself in action, translating the vision into action. For example, you go out and work with the Catholic Workers for a month at a time, then you come back into the monastery and go into hermitage.

Of course, individuals operate on different wave-lengths. Some may go back and forth in rapid succession. Others may do it on a long-term basis, spending a year in a secluded hermitage somewhere in a cave, then immersing themselves in the city for a year or two. Any many will say, "My center of gravity is not in the monastery; it is outside, in my family, in the world, in the society in which I live. But I need the monastery to counterbalance that." Such people may need to spend a week in a monastery every year, in order to find a sense of vision and give meaning to their lives.

Brother David, you titled your most recent book Gratefulness, the Heart of Prayer. *I wonder what you mean my that? How is gratefulness in fact the heart of prayer?*

In the sense in which I'm using it here, prayer is not just saying prayers; it is the activity of religion. "Religion" is one of those strange nouns that has no verb. You can't say, "I'm religioning." I think the word "praying" is the closest equivalent.

At the heart of religion, as I mentioned earlier, is a sense of belonging. And at the heart of gratefulness, in its deepest sense—as when you say "thank you" and really mean it—is an expression of belonging. When you say "thank you." you are really saying, "We belong together." That is why some people find it so difficult to say "thank you"—because they don't want to be obliged. But in a healthy society that's exactly what you want, mutual obligations. Everybody is obliged to everybody else; we all belong together. One way in which we in our culture express that sense of belonging is by saying "thank you."

But behind that custom stands the vast phenomenon of gratefulness, which is an attitude toward life that we can cultivate. We can be alert in each moment to the gift that life is. If we can cultivate that attitude, we're right at the heart of religious living. And that is true prayer: a deep awareness of our limitless belonging—to self, to others, to the universe, to God, to ultimate reality. In fact, the most basic, most universally satisfying definition of God that I can find is "the one to whom we belong." God is the reference point for our deepest sense of belonging. And gratefulness is the joyful living out of that belonging. Every moment can spark that joyfulness in us.

Bernadette Roberts

Bernadette Roberts is the author of three books on Christian contemplation, *The Experience of No-Self, The Path to No-Self,* and *What Is Self?* Roberts began her own spiritual journey in the Roman Catholic cloister, where, as a young nun, she experienced what she calls the "unitive state," the state of oneness with God. After nine years in the convent, she felt called to return to ordinary life to share what she had learned and to take on the problems and experiences of others.

In subsequent years she completed a graduate degree in education, married, raised four children, and taught at the preschool, high school, and junior college levels. At the same time, she continued her contemplative practice.

Then, quite unexpectedly, some 20 years after leaving the convent, Roberts reportedly experienced the dropping away of the unitive state itself and came upon what she calls the experience of no-self—an experience for which, she says, the Christian literature gave her no clear road maps or guideposts. Her books, which combine fascinating chronicles of her own experiences with detailed maps of the contemplative terrain, are an attempt to provide such guideposts for those who follow after her.

Now nearly 60, Roberts still lives in her native Los Angeles, leaving four or five times each year to teach at the "invitation of small groups around the country who are interested in the contemplative life." When not at work on a fourth book, she supports herself as a parttime receptionist and babysitter.

When I contacted her for an interview, Roberts was at first reluctant, protesting that others who had tried had distorted her meaning, and that nothing had come of it in the end. Instead of a live interview, she suggested, why not send her a list of questions to which she would respond in writing, thereby eliminating all possibility of misunderstanding. As a result, I never got to meet Bernadette Roberts face to face until long after our interview—but her answers to my questions, which are as carefully crafted and as deeply considered as her books, are a remarkable testament to the power of contemplation.

Bernadette Roberts

The Path to No-Self

Bernadette, could you talk briefly about the first three stages of the Christian contemplative life as you experienced them—in particular, what you (and others) have called the unitive state?

Strictly speaking, the terms "purgative," "illuminative," and "unitive" [often used of the contemplative path] do not refer to discrete stages, but to a way of travel where "letting go," "insight," and "union" define the major experiences of the journey. To illustrate the continuum, authors come up with various stages, depending on the criteria they are using. St. Teresa, for example, divided the path into seven stages, or "mansions." But I don't think we should get locked into any stage theory; it is always someone else's retrospective view of his or her own journey, which may not include our own experiences or insights. Our obligation is to be true to our own insights, our own inner light.

My view of what some authors call the "unitive stage" is that it begins with the Dark Night of the Spirit, or the onset of the transformation process, when the larva enters the cocoon, so to speak. Up to this point, we are actively reforming ourselves, doing what we can to bring about an abiding union with the divine. But at a certain point, when we have done all we can, the divine steps in and takes over. The transforming process is a divine undoing and re-doing that culminates in what is called the state of "transforming union" or "mystical marriage," considered to be the definitive state for the Christian contemplative.

In experience, the onset of this process is the descent of the cloud of unknowing, which, because his former light has gone out and left him in darkness, the contemplative initially interprets as the divine gone into hiding. In modern terms, the descent of the cloud is actually the falling away of the ego-center, which leaves us looking into a dark hole, a void or empty space in ourselves. Without the veil of the ego-center, we do not recognize the divine; it is not as we thought it should be.

Seeing the divine eye-to-eye is a reality that shatters our expectations of light and bliss. From here on we must feel our way in the dark, and the special eye that allows us to see in the dark opens up at this time. So here begins our journey to the true center, the bottom-most, innermost "point" in ourselves where our life and being runs into divine life and being—the point at which all existence comes together.

This center can be compared to a coin: on the near side is our self, on the far side is the divine. One side is not the other side, yet we cannot separate the two sides. If we tried to do so, we would either end up with another side, or the whole coin would collapse, leaving no center at all—no self and no divine. We call this a state of oneness or union because the single center has two sides, without which there would be nothing to be one, united, or non-dual. Such, at least, is the experiential reality of the state of transforming union, the state of oneness.

How did you discover the further stage, which you call the experience of no-self?

That occurred unexpectedly some 25 years after the transforming process. The divine center—the coin, or "true self"—suddenly disappeared, and without center or circumference there is no self, and no divine. Our subjective life of experiences is over—the passage is finished. I had never heard of such a possibility or happening.

Obviously there is far more to the elusive experience we call self than just the ego. The paradox of our passage is that we really do not know what self or consciousness is, so long as we are living it, or are it. The true nature of self can only be fully disclosed when it is gone, when there is no self. One outcome, then, of the no-self experience is the disclosure of the true nature of self or consciousness. As it turns out, self is the entire system of consciousness, from the unconscious to God-consciousness, the entire dimension of human knowing and feeling-experiencing. Because the terms "self" and "consciousness" express the same experiences (nothing can be said of one that cannot be said of the other), they are only definable in terms of "experience." Every other definition is conjecture and speculation.

No-self, then, means no-consciousness. If this is shocking to some people, it is only because they do not know the true nature of consciousness. Sometimes we get so caught up in the content of consciousness, we forget that consciousness is also a somatic function of the physical body, and, like every such function, it is not eternal. Perhaps we would do better searching for the divine in our bodies than amid the content and experiences of consciousness.

How does one move from "transforming union" to the experience of no-self? What is the path like?

We can only see a path in retrospect. Once we come to the state of oneness, we can go no further with the inward journey. The divine center is the innermost "point," beyond which we cannot go at this time. Having reached this point, the movement of our journey turns around and begins to move outward—the center is expanding outward.

To see how this works, imagine self, or consciousness, as a circular piece of paper. The initial center is the ego, the particular energy we call "will" or volitional faculty, which can either be turned outward, toward itself, or inward, toward the divine ground, which underlies the center of the paper. When, from our side of consciousness, we can do no more to reach this ground, the divine takes the initiative and breaks through the center, shattering the ego like an arrow shot through the center of being. The result is a dark hole in ourselves and the feeling of terrible void and emptiness.

This breakthrough demands a restructuring or change of consciousness, and this change is the true nature of the transforming process. Although this transformation culminates in true human maturity, it is not man's final state. The whole purpose of oneness is to move us on to a more final state.

To understand what happens next, we have to keep cutting larger holes in the paper, expanding the center until only the barest rim or circumference remains. One more expansion of the divine center, and the boundaries of consciousness or self fall away. From this illustration we can see how the ultimate fulfillment of consciousness, or self, is no-consciousness, or no-self. The path from oneness to no-oneness is an egoless one and is therefore devoid of ego-satisfaction.

Despite the unchanging center of peace and joy, the events of life may not be peaceful or joyful at all. With no ego-gratification at the center and no divine joy on the surface, this part of the journey is not easy. Heroic acts of selflessness are required to come to the end of self, acts comparable to cutting ever-larger holes in the paper—acts, that is, that bring no return to the self whatsoever.

The major temptation to be overcome in this period is the temptation to fall for one of the subtle but powerful archetypes of the collective unconscious. As I see it, in the transforming process we only come to terms with the archetypes of the personal unconscious; the archetypes of the collective unconscious are reserved for individuals in the state of oneness, because those archetypes are powers or energies of that state. Jung felt that these archetypes were unlimited; but in fact, there is only one true archetype, and that archetype is Self. What is unlimited are the various masks or roles self is tempted to play in the state of oneness—savior, prophet, healer, martyr, Mother Earth, you name it. They are all temptations to seize power for ourselves, to think ourselves to be whatever the mask or role may be.

In the state of oneness, both Christ and Buddha were tempted in this manner, but they held to the "ground" that they knew to be devoid of all such energies. This ground is a "stillpoint," not a moving energy-point. Unmasking these energies, seeing them as ruses of the self, is the particular task to be accomplished or hurdle to be overcome in the state of oneness.

We cannot come to the ending of self until we have finally seen through these archetypes and can no longer be moved by any of them.

So the path from oneness to no-oneness is a life that is choicelessly devoid of ego-satisfaction; a life requiring heroic, selfless giving; a life of unmasking the energies of self and all the divine roles it is tempted to play. It is hard to call this life a "path," yet it is the only way to get to the end of our journey.

In The Experience of No-Self *you talk at great length about your experience of the dropping away or loss of self. Could you briefly describe this experience and the events that led up to it. I was particularly struck by your statement "I realized I no longer had a 'within' at all. . . . My interior or spiritual life was finished." For so many of us, the spiritual life is experienced as an "inner" life—yet the great saints and sages have talked about going beyond any sense of inwardness.*

Your observation strikes me as particularly astute; most people miss this point. You have actually put your finger on the key factor that distinguishes between the state of oneness and the state of no-oneness, between self and no-self. So long as self remains, there will always be a "center." Few people realize that not only is the center responsible for their interior experiences of energy, emotion, and feeling, but also, underlying these, the center is our continuous, mysterious experience of "life" and "being." Because this experience is more pervasive than our other experiences, we may not think of "life" and "being" as an "interior" experience. Even in the state of oneness, we tend to forget that our experience of "being" originates in the divine center, where it is one with divine life and being. We have become so used to living from this center that we feel no need to remember it, to mentally focus on it, look within, or even think about it. Despite this fact, however, the center remains; it is the epicenter of our experience of life and being, which gives rise to our experiential energies and various feelings.

If this center suddenly dissolves and disappears, the experiences of life, being, energy, feeling, and so on come to an end, because there is no "within" any more. And without a "within," there is no subjective, psychological, or spiritual life remaining—no experience of life at all. Our subjective life is over and done with. But now, without center and circumference, where is the divine?

To get hold of this situation, imagine consciousness as a balloon filled with, and suspended in, divine air. The balloon experiences the divine as immanent, "in" itself, as well as transcendent, beyond or outside itself. This is the experience of the divine in ourselves and ourselves in the divine; in the state of oneness, Christ is often seen as the balloon (ourselves), completing this trinitarian experience. But what makes this whole experience possible—the divine as both immanent and transcendent—is obviously the balloon, i.e., consciousness or self. Consciousness sets up the divisions of within and without, spirit and matter, body and soul, immanent and transcendent; in fact, consciousness is responsible for every division we know of.

But what if we pop the balloon—or, better, cause it to vanish like a bubble that leaves no residue. All that remains is divine air. There is no divine in anything, there is no divine transcendent or beyond anything, nor is there anything in the divine, nor is the divine anything. We cannot point to anything or anyone and say, "This or that is divine." So the divine is all—all but consciousness or self, which created division in the first place.

As long as consciousness remains, however, it does not hide the divine, nor is it ever separated from it. In Christian terms, the divine known to consciousness and experienced by it as immanent and transcendent is called God; the divine as it exists prior to consciousness and after consciousness is gone is called Godhead. Obviously, what accounts for the difference between God and Godhead is the balloon or bubble—self or consciousness. As long as any subjective self remains, a center remains; and so, too, does the sense of interiority.

You mention that, with the loss of the personal self, the personal God drops away as well. Is the personal God, then, a transitional figure in our search for ultimate loss of self?

Sometimes we forget that we cannot put our finger on any thing or any experience that is not transitional. Since consciousness, self, or subject is the human faculty for experiencing the divine, every such experience is personally subjective; thus, in my view, "personal God" is any subjective experience of the divine. Without a personal, subjective self, we could not even speak of an impersonal, non-subjective God; one is just relative to the other. Before consciousness or self existed, however, the divine was neither personal nor impersonal, subjective nor non-subjective—and so the divine remains when self or consciousness has dropped away.

Consciousness by its very nature tends to make the divine into its own image and likeness; the only problem is, the divine has no image or likeness. Hence consciousness, of itself, cannot truly apprehend the divine. Christians (Catholics especially) are often blamed for being the great image makers, yet their images are so obviously naive and easy to see through, we often miss the more subtle, formless images by which consciousness fashions the divine.

For example, because the divine is a subjective experience, we think the divine is a subject; because we experience the divine through our faculties of consciousness, will and intellect, we think the divine is equally consciousness, will, and intellect; because we experience ourselves as a being or entity, we experience the divine as a being or entity; because we judge others, we think the divine judges others; and so on. Carrying a holy card in our pockets is tame compared to the formless notions we carry around in our minds; it is easy to let go of an image, but almost impossible to uproot our intellectual convictions based on the experiences of consciousness.

Still, if we actually knew the unbridgeable chasm that lies between the true nature of consciousness or self and the true nature of the divine, we would despair of ever making the journey. So consciousness is the marvelous divine invention by which human beings make the journey in subjective companionship with the divine; and, like every divine invention, it works. Consciousness both hides the chasm and bridges it—and when we have crossed over, of course, we do not need the bridge any more.

So it doesn't matter that we start out on our journey with our holy cards, gongs and bells, sacred books, and religious feelings. All of it should lead to growth and transformation, the ultimate surrender of our images and concepts, and a life of selfless giving. When there is nothing left to surrender, nothing left to give, only then can we come to the end of the passage—the ending of consciousness and its personally subjective God. One glimpse of the Godhead, and no one would want God back.

How does the path to no-self in the Christian contemplative tradition differ from the path as laid out in the Hindu and Buddhist traditions?

I think it may be too late for me to ever have a good understanding of how other religions make this passage. If you are not surrendering your whole being, your very consciousness, to a loved and trusted personal God, then what are you surrendering it to? Or why surrender it at all? Loss of ego, loss of self, is just a by-product of this surrender; it is not the true goal, not an end in itself. Perhaps this is also the view of Mahayana Buddhism, where the goal is to save all sentient beings from suffering, and where loss of ego, loss of self, is seen as a means to a greater end. This view is very much in keeping with the Christian desire to save all souls.

As I see it, without a personal God, the Buddhist must have a much stronger faith in the "unconditioned and unbegotten" than is required of the Christian contemplative, who experiences the passage as a divine doing, and in no way a self-doing.

Actually, I met up with Buddhism only at the end of my journey, after the no-self experience. Since I knew that this experience was not articulated in our contemplative literature, I went to the library to see if it could be found in the Eastern religions. It did not take long for me to realize that I would not find it in the Hindu tradition, where, as I see it, the final state is equivalent to the Christian experience of oneness or transforming union. If a Hindu had what I call the no-self experience, it would be the sudden, unexpected disappearance of Atman-Brahman, the divine Self in the "cave of the heart," and the disappearance of the cave as well. It would be the ending of God-consciousness, or transcendental consciousness—that seemingly bottomless experience of "being," "consciousness," and "bliss" that articulates the state of oneness. To regard this ending as the falling away of the ego is a grave error; ego must fall away before the state of oneness can be realized. The no-self experience is the falling away of this previously realized transcendent state.

Initially, when I looked into Buddhism, I did not find the experience of no-self there either; yet I intuited that it had to be there. The falling away of the ego is common to both Hinduism and Buddhism. Therefore, it would not account for the fact that Buddhism became a separate religion, nor would it account for the Buddhists' insistence on no eternal Self—be it divine, individual, or the two in one. I felt that the key difference between these two religions was the no-self experience, the falling away of the true Self, Atman-Brahman.

Unfortunately, what most Buddhist authors define as the no-self experience is actually the no-ego experience. The cessation of clinging, craving, desire, the passions, etc., and the ensuing state of imperturbable peace and joy articulates the egoless state of oneness; it does not, however, articulate the no-self experience or the dimension beyond. Unless we clearly distinguish between these two very different experiences, we only confuse them, with the inevitable result that the true no-self experience becomes lost. If we think the falling away of the ego, with its ensuing transformation and oneness, is the no-self experience, then what shall we call the much further experience when this whole egoless oneness falls away? In actual experience there is only one thing to call it, the "no-self experience"; it lends itself to no other possible articulation. Initially I gave up looking for this experience in the Buddhist literature.

Four years later, however, I came across two lines attributed to Buddha describing his enlightenment experience. Referring to self as a house, he said, "All thy rafters are broken now, the ridgepole is destroyed." And there it was—the disappearance of the center, the ridgepole; without it, there can be no house, no self. When I read these lines, it was as if an arrow launched at the beginning of time had suddenly hit a bull's-eye. It was a remarkable find. These lines are not a piece of philosophy, but an experiential account, and without the experiential account we really have nothing to go on. In the same verse he says, "Again a house thou shalt not build," clearly distinguishing this experience from the falling away of the ego-center, after which a new, transformed self is built around a "true center," a sturdy, balanced ridgepole.

As a Christian, I saw the no-self experience as the true nature of Christ's death, the movement beyond even his oneness with the divine, the movement from God to Godhead. Though not articulated in contemplative literature, Christ dramatized this experience on the cross for all ages to see and ponder. Where Buddha described the experience, Christ manifested it without words; yet they both make the same statement and reveal the same truth—that ultimately, eternal life is beyond self or consciousness. After one has seen it manifested or heard it said, the only thing left is to experience it.

You mention in The Path to No-Self *that the unitive state is the "true state in which God intended every person to live his mature years." Yet so few of us ever achieve this unitive state. What is it about the way we live right now that prevents us from doing so? Do you think it is our preoccupation with material success, technology, and personal accomplishment?*

First of all, I think there are more people in the state of oneness than we realize. For everyone we hear about, there are thousands we will never hear about. Believing this state to be a rare achievement can be an impediment in itself. Unfortunately, those who write about it have a way of making it sound more extraordinary and blissful than it commonly is, and so false expectations are another impediment—we keep waiting and looking for an experience or state that never comes.

But if I had to put my finger on the primary obstacle, I would say it is having wrong views of the journey. Paradoxical though it may seem, the passage through consciousness or self moves contrary to self, rubs it the wrong way—and, in the end, will even rub it out. Because this passage goes against the grain of self, it is, therefore, a path of suffering.

Both Christ and Buddha saw the passage as one of suffering, and basically found identical ways out. What they discovered and revealed to us was that each of us has within himself or herself a "stillpoint"—comparable, perhaps, to the eye of a cyclone, a spot or center of calm, imperturbability, and non-movement. Buddha articulated this central eye in negative terms as "emptiness" or "void," a refuge from the swirling cyclone of endless suffering. Christ articulated the eye in more positive terms as the "Kingdom of God" or the "Spirit within," a place of refuge and salvation from a suffering self. For both of them, the way out was first to find that stillpoint and then, by attaching ourselves to it, by becoming one with it, to find a stabilizing, balanced anchor in our lives. After that, the cyclone is gradually drawn into the eye, and the suffering self comes to an end. And when there is no longer a cyclone, there is also no longer an eye.

So the storms, crises, and sufferings of life are a way of finding the eye. When everything is going our way, we do not see the eye, and we feel no need to find it. But when everything is going against us, then we can find the eye. So the avoidance of suffering and the desire to have everything go our own way runs contrary to the whole movement of our journey; it is all a wrong view. With the right view, however, one should be able to come to the state of oneness in six or seven years—years not merely of suffering, but years of enlightenment, for right suffering is the essence of enlightenment.

Because self is everyone's experience underlying all cultures, I do not regard cultural wrong views as an excuse for not searching out right views. After all, each person's passage is his or her own; there is no such thing as a collective passage. So I would say that cultural values cannot block our search or inhibit our passage. I cannot believe that people in Russia or India find the passage any easier than we do, here in the United States. If they do, I'd like to hear about it.

Stephen Levine

Although still in his early 50s, Stephen Levine has faced death countless times. As codirector, with his wife, Ondrea, of the Hanuman Dying Project (a service organization founded by Ram Dass), he spent eight years guiding hundreds of people through the painful and often illuminating journey of terminal illness. In addition, he has counseled hundreds more in the throes of bereavement and reached thousands through his workshops and books on "conscious living and conscious dying."

Yet Levine's face remains boyish and playful, his smile unstintingly warm. Indeed, his heartful presence bears testimony to the principles he teaches: to let go of the holding that separates us from others and to open to the strength and love that lie beneath.

Levine first embarked on the spiritual path in the 1950s, when, as a 19-year-old living in New York City, he became an early student of the American kundalini master Rudrananda (Rudi). From there he worked his way through "heart meditation, psychedelics, and lots of time spent with the *Bhagavad Gita*" to become a student of vipassana meditation in the 1970s. Before long his teachers, Jack Kornfield and Joseph Goldstein, were asking him to teach.

Levine and Ram Dass (Richard Alpert) have been friends since the late '60s, when Alpert and Timothy Leary were the "alchemists of the time," and Levine was the editor of an alternative newspaper called the *San Francisco Oracle*. In the years since, Levine and Ram Dass have led dozens of workshops together and have coauthored a book, *Grist for the Mill*.

It was during a workshop with Ram Dass in 1975 that Levine first encountered Elisabeth Kübler-Ross. "We had a few nice moments," he recalls, "but it was busy, and your time is usually reserved for people who need you the most." About eight months later Levine had the feeling that he and Kübler-Ross "might have some work to do together." As it turns out, she had a similar feeling, and the two were soon coleading workshops in which Levine offered meditation as a tool for being more present and attentive with those who were ill or grieving, and Kübler-Ross gave her now-famous instructions for dealing with death. As yet, however, Levine had never worked with the dying himself.

"Kübler-Ross took me to a patient she was working with at a hospital in Texas," Levine recalls. "And I thought, 'Wonderful! Now I'm going to see a real master at her intuitive process.' We walked into the room, and Elisabeth pulled a chair up to the bed. 'You sit here,' she said, and she went off. At that moment I may have been closer to death than the woman lying in bed.

"All the debris in my mind was clearly evident, all the ego that separates, all the rescue fantasies—and I already had a dozen years of meditation under my belt! This work was clearly a mirror for the things that kept me from God, from my true nature. So work with the dying became work with myself."

As codirector of the Dying Project (he left the post in 1985), Levine ran a hotline that made him accessible round the clock to the dying and their relatives, friends, and caregivers. One simply had to dial the number and either Stephen or Ondrea would respond with advice, a listening ear, and an open heart. Levine has also offered free consultations to hospitals nationwide, has written three books on dying *(Who Dies?, Meetings at the Edge,* and *Healing into Life and Death*), and has adapted his dying meditations for women struggling to heal the wounds of childhood sexual abuse. In addition, he has authored books on ecology (*Planet Steward*), vipassana meditation (*A Gradual Awakening*), and the travails of the spiritual path (*Grist for the Mill*, with Ram Dass). In all his writings the message is the same: If we are to be truly healed, we must learn to let go of our attachments, our expectations, our anger, our fear, and open our hearts to the present moment just as it is.

"At first my primary interest was meditation," says Levine of his own spiritual unfolding. "Then service came along as a means of deepening the meditation and bringing it out into the world. Soon, meditation became primarily something that fed the ability to serve. Now we've come full circle, and we're focusing once again on our own internal processes. Service has helped us see at an even deeper level that the passing show of the mind is simply the passing show of the mind.

"Although our meditations are used by many psychotherapists throughout the country," he adds, "I don't want our work to be considered merely psychological. Psychological work is often necessary for getting the feet more firmly planted on the path of light. But we don't want to get mired in that ball of yarn we call the mind. The work we've done is to take people beyond therapy to the heart of the matter, to the healing we took birth for."

With their children finally grown and out of the house, Stephen and Ondrea have moved to the mountains near Taos, New Mexico, where they are facilitating their own healing by "practicing silence" together. (After several bouts with cancer, Ondrea has rheumatoid arthritis and an undiagnosed second condition which is thought to be either lupus or multiple sclerosis.) Several times each year they emerge from seclusion to give workshops and meet with those who seek their counsel. They are also completing a lengthy manuscript on intimate relationships based on their experience as a couple and their work with others.

The following interview took place at the Miyako Hotel in San Francisco, where Stephen and Ondrea were resting between workshops. Stephen has a remarkable presence: When he smiles, as he does often—the full-bodied, gutsy grin of a streetwise ex-hippie—his face seems to expand toward you and rub up against you, like an affectionate puppy. Yet his eyes are deep, compassionate, soulful, as if he had lived many lifetimes longer than the rest of us. People say they feel loved in his presence, not in some abstract, disembodied way, but fully, from head to toe.

Yet, like the Zen masters of old, Levine is also a trickster. At one point, when the conversation gets too "airy-fairy" for his tastes, he threatens to light up a cigarette (an old addiction) just to "balance things out."

Stephen Levine

The Healing We Took Birth For

I understand that you've studied with a number of spiritual teachers over the years. What is your practice these days?

(Laughs) Right now it's picking up this glass of water, as much as I can. Our meditation practice is *vipassana*, basic Buddhist mindfulness. We do a lot of work with *metta*, lovingkindness meditation. But after so many years, practice doesn't begin with a "p" and end with an "e." It's being present—which means, when you wake up in the morning, to notice the degree of fear and joy, or the mixture of both. To notice, when you roll over in bed, what motivated you to roll over in bed: was it to relieve discomfort? When you step onto the floor, to feel the floor (cold, warm), to notice the mind's response, but to stay in the heart of things. To take birth is our practice.

It's harder to define now than it used to be. We're trained in southern Buddhist practice, but the places we're most often invited to teach are Zen centers and Hindu ashrams. So our connections are clearly not limited to the tradition within which we were trained.

How does all the spiritual work you've done influence your work with the dying?

The spirituality is our work. We don't experience them as separate. What we're really doing is experiencing self confronting that which goes beyond self. And we can do that in something as mundane as stubbing our toe when we walk across the room. When we stub our toe, most of our conditioning sends anger and hatred into the pain. When the body and the mind are most in need of mercy, it's often least available, because we've been conditioned to close around discomfort.

To the degree that we have room in our hearts for our pain, we have room in our hearts for other people's pain. As a result, when we're with someone who's dying, the room may be ripe with suffering and impermanence, but it doesn't block the heart. To the degree that we don't think patients are simply their bodies, we don't reinforce their fear of death. Death is not a tragedy to us. By working with our common everyday grief—we may call it anger or doubt or distrust; all of those states of mind are states of grief, of separation—we become more aware of the heart we share, and this helps us. It brings us more into our hearts. It makes us pay attention. It's the healing we took birth for.

That's really what Ondrea and I are involved in—working with that kind of heartfulness. When you put it into words, you've already created separation and confusion, because it's all so open to interpretation. People say to us, "Gee, it must be such hard work." It isn't. It's the most natural work we could do. It's effortless. We don't have to will it to happen. It's like the difference between effort and energy—we often find that it's just "the Energy," without someone there exerting any effort.

We're taught so much by all of this. People come up to us all the time and say, "It's so wonderful; you helped me so much when my mother died," or "You've given me such support in dealing with AIDS." We have to laugh: We get all the credit, but they're doing all the work. They're the ones who deserve the credit. For us it's really quite simple. I don't know what else we'd do.

Someone once asked Mother Teresa what she'd do if there were no more poor people in the world. "I'd be unemployed," she said. (Laughter)

Well, that's her job.

I understand that you, Ondrea, have had cancer. Is that true?

Ondrea Levine: Yes, twice.

How has that influenced your work together.

Ondrea: It gave us a focus for our healing. And since our priority is the truth, it gave us an opportunity to use each other as an experiment in truth. At first we used my body, trying different techniques for applying lovingkindness and mindfulness to heal it. At other times Stephen's body was imbalanced, so we worked with that. In that sense my illness has been extremely fruitful. It's also where we came to see that, at least in our experience, true healing involves more than just the body.

In your new book, Stephen, you contend that true healing is not really limited to the physical body.

Stephen: Yes, healing may or may not be reflected in the physical body. Some of the most remarkable healings we've seen have been hearts that were hard as stone opening like a flower in the course of dying. I've seen people who healed their body and never experienced that level of healing, who healed their body and still cheat on their wives, still push around their children, still hate. It's nice to be alive, and it's wonderful to have this classroom in which to learn, but we see an awful lot of injury done in the name of healing. A lot of what's called healing is actually the antithesis of the healing we took birth for. It's identification with the body and the personality to such an extent that no one around them can stand to be with them—a healing that intensifies unfinished business instead of completing it.

These people might get better physically . . .

And their world gets smaller and smaller, and their heart stays unsatisfied and disconnected.

In one of your books you mention that those who get healed are usually those who can let go and open to their illness. But research has apparently shown that those who beat their disease are those who fight it the most.

It's very difficult to know what would work for everyone. But let's just imagine, for the sake of argument, that 10 percent of the people, by adroitly cultivating aggression, are able to mobilize their immune system in such a way that they can eradicate cancer from their body. Now what about those other 90 percent who die hating themselves, who die saying, "I'm responsible for my illness, therefore I'm a failure"? We've seen too many people die with their hearts closed to themselves because of ideas whose intention was good.

Holism doesn't go deep enough; it's often a half whole, a half truth. Although some people can use those half truths beneficially to cure some parts of their illness, more people we see are burned terribly by ideas such as, "You choose to live or you choose to die." Well, choice has a lot to do with it, and if you choose to die, chances are you'll hinder your own healing. But, if you die, it doesn't mean you chose to die. If that were so, all the people dying from AIDS would be second-stringers, incompetents, because they can't heal themselves.

I've seen too many 95-year-old widows strapped in wheelchairs in convalescent homes praying every day to die and not dying, in fact, losing their faith in God because God won't take them. Every cell is soaked with a desire to die, but it's not enough. On the other hand, I've seen people who work so hard using every healing practice, techniques that are very difficult for them to undergo, who do everything they can to stay in the body, and still die. They're not failures. And ideas like "You choose to live or you choose to die" are half truths which, taken deeper, can be very valuable, but left on the surface can be very destructive.

The idea that you're responsible for your cancer has caused as much suffering as any idea I've ever encountered. We're not responsible for our cancer; we're responsible *to* our cancer. If you find pain in the body and say "I'm responsible for this pain," then judgment is liable to encircle and encrust that pain, and that very resistance amplifies suffering. But if you're responsible *to* your pain, then you can bring it into your heart. The idea is a useful one, but it doesn't reach the depths where real healing takes place.

I know holistic doctors who, having gotten cancer, have said, "My gracious, I've told people things off the top of my head that now I see aren't so. I have to open my heart to my cancer. I have to be responsible to it. There's no blame. Who knows?" I think "don't know" is far better to work with than causation. I've seen too many saints die of illness. In fact, all of our teachers have died of an illness. Neem Karoli Baba apparently died of heart failure. Nisargadatta, Suzuki Roshi, Ramakrishna, Vivekananda, Ramana Maharshi, of cancer. Korean Zen master Soen Sa Nim, with whom we sometimes teach, has diabetes. Recently his heart went into fibrillation; he was having a heart attack, and his students were very concerned. As they were rushing him to the hospital, he said, "It's OK, you know, my heart is only singing." That may be a heart that's diseased, but that's a heart that's healed.

I can no longer support the idea that illness is bad. Illness is teaching.

You say illness is a teaching. Where does that teaching come from? And what is the message?

Where does it come from? What is the teaching? (Laughs) Where's my Zen stick?

I had a patient say to me once, "You know, cancer is the gift for the person who has everything." This was a beautiful 50-year-old woman who had had both breasts removed. She stood up at one of our workshops and said, "Three years ago I was graced with cancer. I'd looked my whole life for a teacher, and it wasn't until I got cancer that I really started to pay attention to the preciousness of each breath, to the momentum of each thought, till I saw that this moment is all. All my other teachers," she said, "gave me ideas. Cancer caused me to directly experience my life. When I got cancer, it was up to me to get born before I died." You know, very few of us will surrender that much into any of our practices. There's nothing wonderful about suffering, nothing at all, but it gets our attention. And wherever there's attention, there's healing. People have to be relatively advanced in their practice before they will give as much attention to ecstasy as they will to agony.

Where does it come from? Why, to be overly cute, let's just say it's a withdrawal from Karma Savings and Loan. It doesn't matter where it comes from. Buddha said it doesn't matter how long you've forgotten, only how soon you remember. It doesn't matter what yesterday was, it's how you are relating this very instant to the contents of the mind and body, and how open your heart is in the present moment. We don't learn to take the next step by looking back over our shoulder at the last one. If we're in this moment fully, we'll be in the next moment fully. If we're not in this moment, if our life is an afterthought, if we are constantly taking a step and then identifying with the mind's incessant appraisal of how that step was taken, we'll never actually take a step. We'll always have taken a step, and we'll always be two seconds behind ourselves.

We're with people on their deathbed who say, looking back at their life, "What the hell was that all about? I thought life was something that was coming, but it never got here." John Lennon has a line in one of his songs, "Life is what's happening while we're busy making other plans."

Tell me about your work with AIDS. In one sense, AIDS patients are simply other people who are dying. Yet I wonder if there's something unique about working with AIDS patients—something unique in their experience, some unique lesson to be learned.

We'd been working with terminally ill patients for many years, and we thought we'd seen dying. Then AIDS came along. Unique? No, everybody dies, and everybody dies with varying relationships to the density of the mind and the openness of the heart, and they die with whatever work they've done at their fingertips, plus something else, grace or good fortune or whatever it is. Dying brings out the best in us. It also brings out the worst, but I see more purification happening than deeper enmeshment in suffering. Indeed, what we've seen in our work is that most people don't give themselves permission to live until they've been given a terminal diagnosis. It brings out a real acuity of perception.

The whole gay community has been given a death sentence, and it has brought out in them a heart the likes of which we've never experienced before. In all the spiritual communities we've visited in this country, Hindu, Buddhist, Jewish, Sufi, we've never seen such growth, such deepening. The healing within the gay community has been phenomenal. Perhaps the only difference between AIDS patients and others is that no other illness is so inevitably terminal. When people get cancer, they set to work and choose a healing method, and they have hundreds of models, aunts and uncles and mothers and brothers, people who have survived the diagnosis 10, 15, even 20 years. The AIDS group doesn't have that kind of experience yet.

I notice sometimes I'll say "AIDS community," but that's not a good term to use, because it implies that AIDS is a gay disease. Although there's a community at this moment among those who have AIDS, I don't want it to be thought of as the AIDS community because that impugns the gay community as the source of the contagion. In fact, it's suspected that AIDS entered the country through many different doors at the same time.

What about the so-called meaning or message of AIDS? Some people have the idea that AIDS has something to teach us. The popular press seems to see it is as signaling the end of Sodom and Gomorrah, and others believe that AIDS has come to bring spiritual transformation to the world.

Everything is a teaching. AIDS has just brought that to our attention. If we would pay attention to the toast popping out of the toaster, or to our boredom or our anger . . . we can no longer elude the necessity of the healing we took birth for. I'm not particularly interested in meaning, because meaning usually keeps us in our heads, and our healing needs to be directly experienced in our hearts. Meaning is separation. Of course, my mind still finds great solace in the eclair of meaning, but ultimately meaning just interferes with the work that's to be done.

For instance, in a relatively early stage of grief, people will find a lot of meaning in the death of their loved one, because the mind has to go slow before it can sink down into the heart. It needs handholds, rungs on the ladder, this meaning and that meaning, before it can just let go into the "ah" of being. We need to use whatever will bring us into the heart of healing.

Meaning gets our attention, but if we don't practice what we've learned, we can't complete the healing we took birth for. In Zen, even insight, a moment after it has arisen, if held to, is considered a hindrance. All meaning has to be open-ended.

You use the term "the healing we took birth for." What do you mean by that?

I've never met a being whose heart is open all the time, and I've met some extraordinary beings. Those moments when our hearts are closed, which are natural, are ripe opportunities for our heart to be open even to its being closed. Ironically, the further our heart opens, the further it must go to close. So the more open our heart has been, the denser we feel when it's closed. To have mercy on ourselves even when our heart is closed is healing. Not to force it open, because force closes the heart.

The healing we took birth for . . . It's almost like everyone stepped off the elevator and took a number. One person's number is "I'm gay and I have AIDS." Another person's number is "I was sexually abused when I was a child." Someone else's number is "I'm an alcoholic." Someone else's number is "I'm a child of an alcoholic." Everyone has work to do. I don't know anyone who doesn't have some unfinished business with themselves. Finishing that business is the healing we took birth for.

When the Buddha became enlightened, he said, "I've broken the roofbeam." In other words, that which compulsively made me take on a body or a form, that which made me do anything at all, is now absent. I am in the very instant in which creation is unfolding. I am at the very edge of the Big Bang. To come that fully into the moment, where nothing stays our healing and nothing keeps our heart closed, is the healing we took birth for.

We were originally drawn to the whole issue of healing by people who would go from fourth-stage cancer or severely degenerated heart disease to a state in which the body was no longer ill. Then we started to notice that, more than being well, these people were more well than they had ever been before in their lives. Something more than their body had healed. Clearly something profound was going on—psychologically and heartfully these people were in better shape than ever. That was the healing they took birth for. And cancer or AIDS or heart disease brought their attention to it.

We saw the same thing occurring in those who died. We saw people who had lived their lives in separation and judgment and dishonesty and distrust come to a place, through deep inner searching and daily practice, of so much love . . . the sign of that kind of healing was that when they left, they passed the healing on, and all about them were healed. That's what we see happening in the gay community. The healing is being passed on.

In contrast, I see people who heal their body and actually pass the illness on. Everyone in their family feels judged and hated and becomes tense or suicidal. When there's real healing, those around the deathbed are healed as well.

What about meditation or other spiritual practices? Are these helpful for people who are dying?

They help those whose temperaments are suitable. In the beginning, I think, the most useful practice is forgiveness. Anybody who has done any deep spiritual practice knows you inevitably come to a time of hellish holding. Forgiveness helps to soften it—that and whatever other spiritual practice you do. When somebody who has pain in their body sees the unskillfulness of sending hatred and judgment into their pain, they can start to send forgiveness instead and soften around their pain.

For example, when we take medicine, we usually take two pills of medicine and one pill of self-disgust, because we're taking our healing from outside. But when we start to guide medicine into the area of illness, to draw in the healing by opening the pathway with forgiveness and lovingkindness, we start to set up a conduit between the heart and the area of illness, through which the breath of compassion can pass. To open up that passageway, forgiveness for oneself and others can be very useful.

To practice forgiveness doesn't necessarily mean to sit down and do a formal forgiveness practice, although many of the people we work with do just that. Those that don't, however, are still practicing forgiveness. Some of the people we work with take the "high path with no railing," working with something like the "Who am I?" practice recommended by Ramana Maharshi, or the complete choiceless awareness and non-holding of some of the deeper levels of vipassana—letting it all come and letting it all go. But that path is not for everybody. We also work with people whose practice is to sing, because they've never allowed themselves to hear themselves from the heart. They've only heard their mind talking, and when they sing, it opens their heart. Whatever the practice, the point is to see that we're not this body. And the less we're identified with this body, the less death is a trap, and the more the body is open to that experiment in truth that Ondrea was talking about.

What about working with your own grief? Certainly, being close to so many people who've died, you must do quite a lot of grieving yourself.

There again, what a wonderful opportunity to touch our essential separateness, our essential grief. You know, yogis sit for 20 years in caves to touch that. We're allowed the opportunity almost every day. When we're working with a 13-year-old girl who is dying, it reflects our daughter back to us. When we're with a 19-year-old boy who has just left home to go to college—he's so happy to be out of the house, and now he has a brain tumor and has to return home and let his parents take care of him—it just attunes us to our children, and to our grief. My mother died this year, and my father is going into an Alzheimerish state. Clearly, with my parents in their 80s, I knew that death was not far away, and I used to wonder how I would react when they died. I was surprised and pleased to observe that when my mother died, my predominant feeling was gratitude.

In your work with dying people and in your own relationship, working and living so closely together, you've certainly had plenty of opportunity to explore intimacy. What do you see as the challenge for couples today? People seem to be reevaluating what it means to be in relationship. I'm wondering what you've learned.

Ondrea: We see all of this as work on ourselves. As a couple, our priority is the truth, not each other. We try not to let our self-images get in the way of finding out the truth of the moment. We use each other as a mirror for our holding, just as we use the patients we see. And one by-product is that we've become that much more precious to each other, that much more intimate, that much more bonded. Growing up we have all these clichéd, romantic ideas about becoming one. But it seems we really do have the potential to become one, to melt into each other.

Stephen: When your priority's letting go, there's nothing much to keep you separate.

And you come to treasure one another all the more, I imagine, because you realize how rare it is to be in a relationship with someone who shares your commitment to the truth.

Stephen: A fellow conspirator.

Ondrea: Right, or a teacher. If we look at one another as teachers, the relationship becomes exciting, vibrant. Sure, the mind gets offended at times, feelings get hurt—it's painful to be shown where you're holding—but it's just a wisp. We don't let it trip us up. We don't even fight, because the truth is just so much more important to us.

Stepthen: Ram Dass once visited us and shook his head. "You guys," he said, "each have a twenty-four-hour therapist."

We've also come to see that monogamy is a spiritual necessity in relationship. One of our teachers, Neem Karoli Baba, said you can be *brahmacharya* with one person. In other words, you can have the power that celibacy gives by sharing your sexuality with only one person. And we are brahmacharya with each other. In other words, we're not celibate, we're sexual, but I don't even have dreams of other women.

The importance of commitment and monogamy in spiritual work is a very interesting issue. Would you like to say a little more about that.

We all have two hearts. We have an upper heart, and we have a lower heart. We all have two major sets of smooth muscles, this heart in our chest and this heart here in our groin. Many years ago, before safe abortion was available, women used to take ergot as an abortive measure. Ergot is a spasmodic for the smooth muscles of the body, and it would cause the womb to spasm and dislodge the embryo. But if dosages weren't correctly titrated to the individual, a woman would sometimes have heart palpitations.

About six or seven years ago, a young woman came up to us and said, "I have no more room in my heart now than I had in my vagina when I was two years old and my father raped me." Instantly we realized that everybody has two hearts, and that for many of us the upper heart has become inaccessible because the lower heart has been closed through rough handling or disconnectedness.

In the commune of sexuality and commitment, the lower hearts can open and touch with love. We talk about healing as the ability to touch with love that which has been touched before with hardness and judgment. To be able to touch with the lower heart, to be able to touch sexually with the heart instead of the mind . . . Usually during sex there's so much else going on: we're thinking about the laundry list, about work, about what happened yesterday. We're still caught in the mind, there's still someone and someone. But the moments when we are making love and I literally cannot tell whether we are male or female—those are the most remarkable times. When she is penetrating me. When the lower hearts are so open that there isn't male and female, or male and male, and it isn't even sex.

I don't want to make this sound too highfalutin and abstract, or to make us sound better than we are. But when the lower hearts can touch in love, then the upper hearts become accessible to each other. If the lower hearts cannot touch in love, there's less chance of there being an open and growing relationship between the upper hearts. Now, two people can have a nonsexual relationship and still have their lower hearts and upper hearts meet perfectly. It just means that there's no obstruction, no blockage, no separation.

Would you say that these hearts are the equivalent of the second and fourth chakras?

More important, more outstanding, more essential than two out of seven. Primal being, essential being. In relationship, first the lower hearts come to meet, and in the lower hearts' meeting is all our conditioning. Some psychologists say that when two people are in bed, there are actually six people, the two lovers and both their parents. Well, when there can be the whole world in bed, or no one at all . . . The contact of the lower hearts stirs up all our stuff, and because of that, monogamy is absolutely essential, because without it we wouldn't stay around to face what arises, we'd go find someone else to be sexual with.

Ram Dass

Ram Dass appears for our interview right on schedule, and without entourage. No fanfare. No pretense. No teacherly airs. The physical form has changed over the years, and the tired eyes, incipient pot belly, and silvery hair (what's left of it) indicate that, as he nears 60, Ram Dass is no stranger to the wear and tear that come with age. (Questioned later about how he maintains his physical health, he replies frankly, "I don't have that act together, really.")

Casually but elegantly dressed, without beard now (only the moustache remains), Ram Dass seems relaxed as he makes himself at home in my rather spartan Berkeley, California, office. As we exchange pleasantries and then settle down to address deeper issues, I'm impressed by his sincerity, his no-nonsense willingness to air all—even the most embarrassing personal insights and anecdotes.

This man, I marvel to myself, has been pioneer, spokesperson, fellow traveler, and teacher to a generation of spiritual seekers. His groundbreaking experiments with LSD (when he was still Richard Alpert, a psychology professor at Harvard) set the stage for the psychedelic '60s. And his immensely popular *Be Here Now*, the fruit of his discipleship with the Indian guru Neem Karoli Baba, has guided thousands in their search for spiritual awakening.

In the influential books that followed, Ram Dass chronicled with remarkable candor the triumphs and travails of his own journey of awakening. And throughout, far from becoming a guru himself, he has remained the perpetual student, the perpetual researcher of the realms of the spirit, still experimenting, still exploring a variety of methods—and still reporting his findings to a worldwide following.

In 1989 Ram Dass moved his center of operations from the East Coast, where he had settled to care for his elderly father, to the San Francisco Bay area. Still actively involved in the Seva Foundation, a service organization he founded, he recently facilitated a videotaped series of classes entitled *Reaching Out*, which teach and help catalyze compassionate action. The course is scheduled for broadcast on PBS in 1993. As always, Ram Dass continues to barnstorm the country giving talks and workshops in his own eclectic blend of Hinduism and Buddhism, and he "works extensively with the AIDS community."

RAM DASS

A Gradual Awakening

What is your day-to-day practice like? I know that Neem Karoli Baba (Maharaj-ji) was your original teacher and that under his guidance your practice was primarily devotional. But I also know that you've explored other paths.

My primary practice is *guru-kripa*, the method of the guru, which involves maintaining a somewhat continuous dialogue with him. I carry his presence inside me all the time, and I relate to him about every situation. Eventually this method expands to the point where every experience you have is part of your dialogue with the guru, and life becomes a series of messages or situations being sent to you through which you can get closer. For example, I may see that you are Maharaj-ji in drag, or that he set this scene up to play with me in some way, or that he's standing behind me giggling, reminding me not to take myself too seriously.

In addition, his instructions to me (which are now nearly twenty years old) to feed and serve people, and the fact that his lineage in the Hindu tradition is Hanuman [the monkey god who lives only to serve Ram], leads me to constantly be exploring the ways in which service can be the form of bhakti yoga that brings me closer to freedom.

I just spent two months in Burma sitting in vipassana meditation—that's part of my *sadhana* too. And in a way vipassana brings me closer to Maharaj-ji, because the quieter I am, the more clearly I can hear his teachings. Maharaj-ji himself used to say to me, "Bring your mind to one point and you'll know God."

Part of your practice, then, is to see each situation as an opportunity to get closer to your guru, to see it as his lila, *his play, his teaching.*

He is no longer that guy in India. Now it's at the point where, as Ramana Maharshi used to say, "God, guru, and One are the same." Getting closer to the guru, at this point, means getting closer to my own true self, to the indescribable.

In addition, I sense that in the Hanuman lineage it has never been clearly enunciated exactly what is meant by doing service as a vehicle for awakening. I've always done lots of service, like lecturing, teaching, working with people who are sick or dying, but then I would go meditate in order to cool myself out. I became interested in why I couldn't do the service itself as the vehicle for getting cooled out. Why did I have to rely on *dhyana* yoga (meditation) rather than karma yoga? Why couldn't karma yoga be complete unto itself? So when I came back from Burma, I decided to throw myself into service as hard as I could. I just kept saying yes: I'm taking care of my father, I'm working with AIDS people, I'm working with dying people, I'm teaching aging, I'm doing individual therapy, I help run the Seva Foundation—just more and more stuff, just "yes, yes, yes." And I'm learning where the toxicities are. My sadhana now is examining how I get caught in service, how the grabbing starts, where I lose the injunction of the *Bhagavad Gita* that says, "To do pure Dharma, don't identify with the actor or the fruits of the action."

You're pushing yourself to an edge, then, in the context of service?

Yes, I always do that. I want to see if it works—and if it doesn't, I want to find out why. I want to see where I have to clean up my act so it will work. I know it's possible because Hanuman did nothing but serve Ram, and he had this incredible energy because of the purity of his service. So I'm just examining my impurities, if you will, discovering where I have to tune up my *yana*, my vehicle.

Where do you draw the line? For example, why sleep? Why eat? Why eat as much as you do? Where does one stop giving out completely and start taking care of oneself? Is there a limit?

Even that distinction—taking care of oneself versus giving to others—is a model that gets in the way. If it's working right, when you're giving out, you're also taking care of yourself. My book *How Can I Help?* focuses on how it works both ways. If it doesn't, something is wrong. Through service you should be getting fed, getting energized, becoming lighter and more spacious.

Of course, all this is theoretical. Part of it works for me and part of it doesn't. What I need to do is to keep zeroing in on the part that doesn't and keep explaining it to myself and to everybody else until we can see why, because I'm sure service can be a pure *upaya* (method for achieving enlightenment). I just don't know yet how to articulate it, and I can't find the books that do.

In other words, it's not that there's something wrong with serving so selflessly, but rather that there's something wrong with the vehicle doing the serving that needs to be taken care of.

Exactly. And it's a fascinating adventure for me, because I feel I'm getting closer to my lineage, which is Hanuman and Maharaj-ji. Maharaj-ji used to sleep two hours a night. The rest of the time he would be surrounded by people; he would be yelling and teaching and throwing people out and feeding people and doing whatever he did, and maybe he was doing that on other planes in the room as well—I don't know. In

Burma we didn't eat after 11 in the morning and I found that I slept much less. The fact that we slept four hours a night didn't bother me in the least. Of course, I had very little stimulation out there, and very little attachment. Attachment is what creates the fatigue. Now I sleep maybe 5 1/2 to 6 hours, and then I can't sleep anymore. I get tired sometimes, but I watch why I'm getting tired and what the tiredness brings up in me.

You mentioned your relationship to Maharaj-ji. I think it was Da Free John who said, "Dead gurus don't kick ass." Do you feel that not having a living teacher has been a shortcoming in your practice?

I would love a teacher who would kick ass . . . yes, if I found someone whose truth I trusted enough to give him that license. I miss that in Maharaj-ji. But I don't think it's true that he doesn't kick ass continuously. If you're trying to awaken, life situations kick ass very fast because you keep seeing where you're falling flat on your face again and again. You say, "I have no attachment to power" and then you see yourself going after it like a whore. You have no choice but to face it. That's what kicking ass means—it just shows you where you're stuck. Of course, I would like somebody who could cut through my trips quickly.

But I also see that I don't have a violence about my sadhana the way I used to. I used to have the attitude that it had to be done yesterday, and I was going to get enlightened tomorrow—the drugs were violent, the teachers who would do it to me were violent, the methods were violent. I don't have that attitude anymore. I've developed patience, a sense of timing, and the sense that it's all going fine. I don't think I'm falling off the path. I feel a deepening harmony. The melodrama of sadhana just doesn't interest me anymore.

The Tibetan Buddhist teacher Chogyam Trungpa, defines ego as struggle. Struggle on the path is a kind of ego as well. More and more we need to drop away that sense of struggle.

Exactly.

What about drugs? I understand that even now you do drugs occasionally. How do you see the role of drugs on the path? Do you see your occasional drug use as a weakness, or is it just not a problem for you, particularly?

Of those two options, I would choose the latter. It's not a weakness, by any means. I see chemicals as an *upaya*, a method, that we only know how to use in a certain limited way. When my guru took acid and nothing happened, he said, "Yogis used these kinds of things years ago, but they used them in conjunction with fasting and so on. Nowadays, people don't know how to use them." That's what I experience—that people don't know how to use them. They're usable, but they are not a total upaya. He said, "It allows you to have *darshan* with the saints. But it would be better to be Christ than to visit him. This won't do that for you." I hear that very clear, subtle distinction. It's as if the drug experience gives you an astral analogue rather than the thing itself.

At the same time, I incredibly honor what psychedelics have done for me. I would be a complete phony if I found it efficacious to reject them at this point. However, they have become less and less interesting to me as the years have gone on—irrelevant, if you will. I take them now and then because just the irrelevance makes my setting for using them better than when I believed that I needed them and felt they were going to take me somewhere.

In a way I'm still a research scientist of psychedelic chemicals. I feel like I have a responsibility to that upaya, just as I have a responsibility to Hanuman and to meditation, to understand them clearly and be able to communicate to others the ways they work. When a chemical comes along, unless it's very violent, I will try it and see what it has to say.

The other thing about drugs is that for a number of years I would invaribly take a puff of a joint before I lectured. The reason I did this was that I always assumed the audience wanted me to be higher than they were. That's what they came for—for me to get them high.

Your definition of high was . . .

Where my mind would be more liquid and playful and spacious than theirs. Since getting up in front of a large lecture can be constricting from an ego point of view, I would override it with a puff of a joint. I found over the years that I would never smoke alone—it just doesn't interest me—but I would do it for the audience. I used to kid that one puff could get 3,000 people high.

Then I began asking myself, "Why do I assume people want me to be different than I am? Why can't I just be who I am? If they don't like it, they won't come to the lectures. And if they don't come to the lectures, I'll do something else." It was scary, but I decided to do it, because I felt heavy, and thick, and caught in my ego. I was under the impression that my speaking was better when I was high, but I realized that it wasn't the performance that changed, it was my evaluation of the performance. When I smoked, I was less judgmental and more appreciative of myself. All I had to do was deal with the judging factor rather than assuming that the performance had to change. So I did a tour absolutely straight, and I never had such a wonderful time in my life. The audience was so responsive. I stayed in people's homes because I no longer had that kind of private world to protect. All the paranoia was gone.

When I was in Burma doing vipassana meditation, I experienced that the way I used drugs and the way I used my guru were similar in certain ways. They were both—not totally, but in part—a reflection of my psychodynamic needs. I was using both the drugs and the guru, saying, "I can't do it—you do it for me." There was a certain feeling of inadequacy, of dependency. And I saw that my way of using the guru was keeping me from merging with the guru, because I was keeping that distance out of my own psychological need. As I explored what that was about, I experienced my fear of power—I've always said in the past that when I get it, I misuse it, so I've always mistrusted myself with power. Because [I believed] I would become arrogant, cold, manipulative. . . .

I hear an ambivalence toward power.

Exactly. I loved it, I was afraid of it, and I hated my love of it, because my love of it was impure in my own eyes. And I suddenly realized that the Theravadin (vipassana) tradition was the path of the warrior, and the warrior is someone who accepts his own power. That's why I had such a hard time with the concept of right effort in Buddhism. I kept saying, "What effort?"

I remember once going to see Trungpa Rinpoche when he was lecturing at Tail of the Tiger in Vermont. I was waiting out in a field in a VW, smoking grass with some friends, and someone came up and said, "Trungpa wants to see you." I went up to his room, and Trungpa was sitting on a chair with a sake bottle in front of him. He said, "Ram Dass, we have to accept responsibility." And I said, "What responsibility? God has all the responsibility, I don't have any responsibility. 'Not my will, but Thy Will, oh Lord.'" And he said, "Ram Dass, you're copping out." That stuck with me for a long time.

You mentioned psychological need and psychodynamics. What about psychotherapy—your own psychotherapy in particular? I understand that you were recently a client in psychotherapy, and I'm wondering how you see psychotherapy as a skillful means in conjunction with spiritual practice.

Individual psychodynamics distort and color—and, if you will, define the boundaries of—the way a sadhana can work. People meditate for lots of different reasons psychologically, and those psychological reasons ultimately define the boundaries of their practice, unless the method takes them beyond their original motivation for using the method.

For example, people who have a difficult time in social relationships may find the monastic life appealing. Or people who have very strong sexual desires may be drawn to tantra. But the fact that their practice of tantra is based on their sexual desire starts to limit the way in which they can understand tantra, because at some point, tantra has to go beyond sexual desire.

The same with people who are prone to a monastic life—they may be caught in the monastic style and be unable to see that they also have to integrate their more social, extraverted side.

Exactly. Because as long as you push anything away, it has you. As long as you have a model of why you are doing something, the model defines the boundaries of what you do. The model is like a prison of the

Light. Lots of people, for example, serve out of a sense of righteousness, which is based on guilt and inadequacy. That defines the limits of their service as a sadhana. True service and compassion have nothing to do with righteousness.

When you see that psychology plays such a key role in spiritual practice, it behooves you to attend to your psychodynamics at some point. But I don't think it's reasonable to expect your therapist to be your spiritual teacher also; I think you have to learn to use therapists without buying their whole reality principle. I was a psychotherapist for many years, and I was [a client] in Freudian analysis many years ago. When I went into spiritual work, I said, in effect, "The spiritual practices are a meta game, and they will ultimately dissolve all the psychological stuff."

Then I got involved with this being Emmanuel, who speaks through Pat Rodegast. Emmanuel's a wonderful friend, a lovely guy. I asked him, "Emmanuel, what should I be doing?" And he said, "Why don't you try being human? You enrolled in a school, why don't you try taking the curriculum?" It was funny, because I had never thought of my humanity as a practice. I was too busy trying to become divine.

Emmanuel focused me back on my humanity as a path. I realized then that I had work to do in relationships, and I soon found myself in a painful relationship. I was like a 13-year-old boy again; I had stopped my development at a certain stage and just gone ahead in my intellectual and spiritual work. So I decided to go back into therapy for a while—not because I expected the therapist to help me spiritually, but because the psychodynamic level was a veil, and I wanted a veil specialist. And I got one—I got a very good mirror who showed me stuff. And it worked for a while, until it became apparent that I was freer than he was and that there was a point where I really couldn't go any further because I understood what he was mirroring. So I stopped, and we became good friends.

In other words, you were able to second-guess him.

Yes, I knew his trip.

I'm wondering how being a public figure, a representative of a generation, of a movement, has hindered your spiritual practice?

It's hard for me to know how it's been a hindrance, because I have it—power, that is. I don't know what I would be like without it. I can see that it has confronted me with my own attachments, so in that way it's been incredibly graceful. At first I wanted it, then I saw how empty it was, then I got despairing, and it kept changing and changing until now I do what I do, just like someone who sits at his computer all day. The love just pervades all of it; the dynamics of fame are totally irrelevant. They just don't do anything to me anymore.

You mentioned in an interview I read recently that you feel paranoid around people you can charm, because they don't know the real you. You mentioned it in relation to the vipassana teacher U Pandita, whom you were unable to charm.

If you have a very strong symbolic value in society—you're very beautiful, or very rich, or very well-known—people are so busy responding to the symbol that you could starve to death before they would give you what you needed. I was just talking to a man two days ago who had a great deal of political power in the world at one time. He said that before that, he'd go to a party and everyone would ignore him. After that, he'd go to a party and everyone would want to sleep with him. And he hadn't changed. I get that same feeling. A lot of people in public life end up withdrawing and having a few friends they feel safe with, who know them. I don't go in that direction at all. I'm learning how to let people run through their projections. For example, if somebody comes up and says, "Oh, Guru-ji, . . ." well, I'm not a guru, but if I don't push them away, and I don't grab onto them, they can go through their projection much faster than if I had any reaction at all.

Of course, I'm very fortunate because the image that's usually projected onto me is a positive one. After all, what does Ram Dass represent? Someone who's trying to be honest, trying to be spiritual. I'm surrounded by a sea of love, if you will, because people know I don't have any powers, I'm not going to heal them or cure them. I sit on airplanes and answer my mail—I write every answer myself—but over the years the payoff has been incredible; the web of intimate one-on-one contacts just keeps growing. There are people who, when they think of me, feel loving and feel that we are joined together in a journey of spirit. I'm getting a tremendous amount of support from that.

A couple of years ago you stopped making public appearances for a while. I'm wondering why you did that.

Well, I got extremely good at what I was doing, but it wasn't good enough. I had as full a lecture schedule as I could handle, with files full of invitations and people who were very appreciative of my lectures, and I was charging very little and everything was going fine, but I wasn't free. Then I'm just transmitting more suffering, and that isn't good enough. So I decided to stop and give myself however long it took until I could be in public from a different place. I stopped for two years. I had no plan about how long it would last; I sort of assumed it would go on for years. When I stopped, I didn't even know what I would do. It wasn't as if I stopped to do something—I stopped to not do something. I wasn't desperately looking. I was just slowing down and tuning and opening. I started to read more and sit and look out at the marsh near the house I live in.

My work with the Seva Foundation brought me back into lecturing. Also the appreciation I get, when I go into deep enough meditation practice, that service is my way. And also the realization I had last summer that people don't need me to be a finished product, that as long as I am honest, they can take what they can get and use it, and we can share what we have together.

Something really profound happened to me in Burma. I don't even know what it is yet. Before, when I kept talking all the time about this stuff, I'd end up only knowing what I had said, and all I would know about Maharaj-ji were the stories I told about him. I realized I was conceptualizing the universe, and I'd lost Maharaj-ji into the conceptual processes I'd imposed upon him. So I had to shut up for a while to reconnect to the nonconceptual universe.

Now I'm not attached to my words like I was before—it's not the same. Something is different. I'm much more afloat. I'm walking into situations empty now, and the situations create a form. In the form I do what I do, I walk out of the situation, and it's all as empty as it was before.

What Suzuki Roshi calls burning yourself up in each activity and leaving no trace. Before, you were suffering under the burden of your own traces.

Exactly.

How do you think your work with U Pandita in Burma helped effect this change? Was it the moment-to-moment mindfulness, which allowed you to stay with thoughts as they arose?

I think that's certainly a component, but more of it is the kind of peace that's connected with spaciousness. I'm at peace now in some way that makes me not need to define myself in terms of the words I just said. Often, after a situation, I would rehearse what had happened, either to savor it or to be embarrassed anew by some stupid thing I had done. That doesn't happen now at all. I think some of it has to do with being comfortable in that warrior role—or perhaps "peace-ior role" would be a better way to describe it.

One last question, Ram Dass. I'm wondering about the name change. For a while there it seemed that you had gone back to Richard Alpert, but lately, as I understand it, you have become Ram Dass again.

Originally when I got the name Ram Dass, it was a reminder of what my business was, because it means "servant of God." It got people treating me somewhat as a spiritual person, which was a support to my practice.

Then, as the years went by, I began to feel stronger in my faith and connectedness with the spirit, and I saw that the name was an obstacle to my being heard by a large segment of the society that distrusted any Westerners with an Eastern name. So I attempted to go back to my Western name, feeling that I didn't need "Ram Dass" anymore.

However, it was deeper into my consciousness and the cultural consciousness than I had expected. People, I found, really resisted my changing. And I realized that, for my part, I didn't care. Who I am is not a name. Or, as they say of the Tao, "The Great Way has no name." So I decided to "let it be."

S. N. Goenka

Next to the Dalai Lama, S. N. Goenka may be the Asian Buddhist teacher best known in the West. Several prominent American teachers have studied with him; he makes periodic visits to Europe, Australia, and the United States; and hundreds flock each year from all over the world to attend his 10-day and one-month meditation courses near Bombay.

Yet Goenka, though he claims to teach what the Buddha taught, does not call himself a Buddhist. "The Dhamma is universal and non-sectarian," he insists. In a country torn by differences of caste and belief, this ecumenical message is like salve on an open wound. Hindu temples, Christian churches, Buddhist retreat centers, and a Muslim mosque have hosted his meditation courses, and hundreds of Christian priests, monks, and nuns have studied with him as a required part of their pastoral training.

What Goenka imparts to his students is called *vipassana*, often translated as insight meditation. Learned from the great Burmese master U Ba Khin, Goenka's version of this ancient technique emphasizes three aspects: moral behavior, to encourage the mind to settle; mastery of the mind through concentration on the breath; and vipassana proper, purification of the mind through insight into one's physical and mental structure.

Following in the Buddha's footsteps, Goenka claims that this is a direct path to eradicating the threefold source of all suffering: craving, aversion, and ignorance.

Nothing about Goenka's own upbringing would seem to have prepared him to be a teacher of vipassana. Born to an Indian family that had settled in Burma two generations before, Goenka was taught the elaborate rites and rituals of conservative Hinduism. As a youth he was groomed to enter the family textile business, which he did while still in his teens, and by his mid-20s he had become an extremely successful businessman and a leader of the Indian community in Burma.

But success brought with it "a lot of ego, a lot of tension," he says, and he began to suffer from severe migraine headaches, for which no cure could be found except morphine. Afraid of becoming an addict, Goenka sought medical care in Europe, America, Japan, but to no avail. Then a friend suggested he take a 10-day vipassana course with U Ba Khin, who, in addition to being a meditation master, held high government office as the accountant-general of Burma.

"I was hesitant initially," Goenka recalls, "partially because I could not believe this meditation could help when the best doctors could not, and partially because it was Buddhist, and I come from a very staunch Hindu family." But meeting U Ba Khin changed his mind.

"He was such a saintly person. The atmosphere around him was so calm and serene, just meeting him for a few minutes persuaded me to give this technique a try." The results were dramatic, and thoroughly convinced Goenka of the value of vipassana.

"Of course, it gave me relief for my migraine. But the biggest relief was that the stress and strain and tension that I used to build up because of my ego—all that got released." Once a "short-tempered person," Goenka found that he now got along much better with his family and staff. Dogmas and rituals became "trivial" as he came to see that the Dhamma is not a religion but an "art of living, the art of living peacefully and harmoniously within oneself and of generating nothing but peace and harmony for others."

For the next 14 years, Goenka practiced regularly with U Ba Khin—when he wasn't attending to the responsibilities of business and family. Then in 1969 he moved to India, where, with the encouragement of his teacher, he began teaching courses in vipassana. Since 1976, Goenka has been based at the Vipassana International Academy in Igatpuri, near Bombay. Built entirely with the donations of grateful students, this center boasts a meditation hall that seats over 400, with individual meditation cells for over 250. Centers have also been established near three other Indian cities and in Nepal, Australia, New Zealand, Japan, England, France, and the U.S. In all, over 100 assistant instructors authorized by Goenka teach this approach without charge or personal profit to all who request it.

A teddy bear of a man in his 60s, Goenka gives every impression of being the "real thing"—one who has faithfully followed the path he espouses and has achieved the happiness and equanimity of which he speaks. During our interview, his voice never betrays the slightest agitation, exuberance, irritation, or concern. Rather, it exudes the quiet, steady warmth and serenity one would expect of a master of one of the world's oldest forms of meditation.

S. N. Goenka

Master of Meditation

In a recent interview, you are quoted as saying, "To me, Hinduism and Buddhism are both madness."

One thing is clear: For me, Dhamma is universal; it can never be sectarian. The life of morality [*sila*] cannot be a monopoly of Hindus or Buddhists or Christians. All must live a moral life, doing nothing at the physical or vocal level to harm other beings.

Nor can mastering the mind [*samadhi*] and keeping it pure and free from all negativities [*panna*; pronounced "pahn-ya"] be a monopoly of any sect or religion. These three [sila, samadhi, and panna] are what constitute the Dhamma, the teachings of the Buddha. So the Dhamma is universal. When I teach this approach, I don't call it Buddhist, because "Buddhism" is a loaded word, like Hinduism, Jainism, Christianity. It refers to a sect, whereas what I am teaching is universal. For me, sects divide; Dhamma unites. When I used the word "madness," I was referring to the situation in India and Sri Lanka, where Hindus are killing Buddhists, and Buddhists are killing Hindus. Even beautiful Dhamma has turned into a sect and become poisonous and fanatical, and the essence of Dhamma has been lost. When one is teaching pure Dhamma, there can't be any madness.

Could you say a little more about the Dhamma? What is this Dhamma you teach?

The Dhamma is the law of nature which governs the entire universe, both animate and inanimate. If one understands the laws of nature and works in accord with them, one leads a good and proper life. Now, Dhamma wants us not to kill, not to steal, not to tell lies, not to engage in sexual misconduct, and not to get intoxicated [the five basic precepts for lay Buddhists]. At the surface level these are actually laws of society, rather than laws of nature, because they contribute to the peace and harmony of society.

But when you start practicing vipassana, deep inside you understand that every time you break any of these precepts, even before you harm others, you have started harming yourself. You can't kill without generating a lot of anger or hatred in your mind. And as soon as you generate hatred or ill will, indeed any negativity, nature starts punishing you, and you become miserable. When you generate anger, you can't possibly experience peace and harmony; you feel so agitated, so miserable.

Similarly, every precept that is broken creates agitation in the mind and makes one miserable. Maybe nature continues to punish us after death; I believe it does. But nature definitely punishes us here and now. This is the law. I place my hand in the fire, and it burns. If I want to keep myself free from burning, I had better keep myself away from the fire. So sila [morality or precepts] is practiced not just to oblige the society, but for one's own sake, to keep oneself peaceful and harmonious.

When these negativities are removed and the mind becomes calm, quiet, and pure, the law of nature is such that a pure mind naturally becomes filled with love, compassion, goodwill. One does not have to cultivate these virtues deliberately; they develop quite naturally. And as soon as I develop love, compassion, and goodwill in my mind, nature starts rewarding me then and there. I feel so peaceful, so harmonious. The reward for a pure mind and the punishment for an impure mind are universal. It works the same for Buddhists, Hindus, Christians, Jews. Because I call myself a Buddhist, nature will not favor me. The Dhamma is universal.

Another way in which Dhamma is universal is that, in the practice of samadhi, controlling or concentrating the mind, the object of concentration is the breath. No verbalization, no recitation of a name or mantra, no visualization of a god or goddess. Just natural breath that comes in and goes out. Now, this too can be practiced without any difficulty by a Hindu, a Muslim, a Christian, or a Jain. Breath is breath. It's a natural reality that is present in every being.

In the practice of panna [wisdom] as well, we observe how mind and matter work, how they interact. When we generate negativity, an unpleasant sensation arises in the body and we become miserable. When we come out of that negativity, we start experiencing peace, and we start helping others because we are being helped ourselves. All this can be done easily by a person of any sect, because no dogma or philosophy or symbolism is involved, just the law of nature. You are just observing nature, which is the same for everyone. So, in my own experience of all three aspects, sila, samadhi, and panna, I have found that Dhamma is universal.

Much of what you have been describing sounds like the law of karma, the law of cause and effect. If this law is indeed universal, I wonder why all the different religions don't teach it.

Not only other religions, but Buddhism as well. Over the centuries the teachings of Buddha have also been corrupted, and the various Buddhist sects have started giving importance to rites, rituals, sectarian beliefs, dogmas, and all kinds of different philosophies.

But the essence of Dhamma is always universal. If the essence of

Dhamma is lost, then every teaching degenerates into sectarian belief. We can't blame any one religion only. Every religion has degenerated into an empty shell; the essence of Dhamma has been lost everywhere. But if we understand what the essence of Dhamma is, then there is no difference between one religion and another. Large numbers of people come to my vipassana courses from different religions, and they find it so beneficial. At the end of one course, a Christian priest told me that I am teaching Christianity in the name of Buddha. At the end of another, a Jain monk said, "This is the essence of our teaching, which we have lost. This is what we are looking for." Hindus, Jews, Muslims, they all say the same thing, because nobody can find any defect in pure Dhamma. It is always acceptable by one and all.

Could you say a little about the four noble truths.

Again, these are so universal. Nobody can deny the first noble truth, the reality of suffering. Association with undesirables [undesirable objects, people, situations] and disassociation from desirables brings suffering. So the first noble truth, the truth of suffering or misery, is universal. The second noble truth, the cause of misery, looks different from the inside and from the outside. It seems that I am miserable because something happened outside that I didn't want to happen, or something didn't happen according to my wishes. But deep inside, everyone can realize that the misery I am suffering is caused by my reaction of craving or aversion. I like something, and I generate craving. I dislike something, and I generate aversion. This second noble truth is common to all.

So, too, the way to come out of misery is common to all, because you have to eradicate the root of your misery, where craving and aversion start. At a gross level, a good way to do that is to practice sila—that is, don't perform any action, physical or verbal, that will disturb or harm other beings, because simultaneously it will harm you. Then work with samadhi; control your mind. But mere control is not sufficient; you must go deep and purify your mind. Once it is purified, craving and aversion are gone, and you have reached the stage where there is no misery at all. It's all so scientific; people accept it so easily. Of course, if we keep fighting over dogma, difficulties arise. But I say, just practice and see: Are you suffering or not? Isn't this the cause of the suffering? And isn't it eradicated by practicing in this way?

You talk about vipassana meditation. What are the techniques of vipassana, as you teach it?

The technique of vipassana is to observe the truth of suffering within oneself, how one becomes agitated, irritated, miserable. One has to go deep within oneself to observe it objectively. Otherwise, the cause of misery always appears to be outside. Say, for example, that I'm angry, and I want to investigate this anger. Even if I close my eyes and try to understand it, the apparent external cause of the anger will keep coming to mind, and I will keep justifying my behavior. "So and so abused me, so and so insulted me, and that's why I am angry. It's no fault of mine." But the fact is, I am miserable.

The technique of vipassana teaches you just to observe. If you are miserable, just observe misery as misery. As you start observing, the cause of misery becomes clear. Because you reacted with negativity, with craving or aversion, you are now experiencing a very unpleasant sensation in the body. But as you keep observing that sensation, it loses its strength and passes away, and the negativity passes with it.

We start with respiration because the mind doesn't become concentrated unless it has an object to focus on. For the first three days of retreat, we observe the breath coming and going at the entrance of the nostrils. As the mind calms down a bit, we start experiencing the sensations around the nostrils and then expand to experience the sensations throughout the body. These sensations take us to the root of our minds. They take us to the root of the misery, to the root of the cause of the misery, and they help us to eradicate that cause. This is what is taught in vipassana.

If I'm not mistaken, the technique of observing the sensations throughout the body is called "sweeping."

Yes, sweeping in the sense that, at a certain stage, all the solidity of the body dissolves. The apparent truth of the material body is solidity. We feel a solid body. But, as you keep observing it objectively, this solidity starts dissolving, and you start experiencing that the entire material structure is nothing but a mass of sub-atomic particles arising and passing away, arising and passing away. The entire body is just a mass of vibration. At first, however, when you are still with the solidity, you can't sweep, can't get a flow of vibration throughout the body, because there are blockages here and there—pain, pressure, heaviness. Instead, you keep observing part by part, and little by little all that solidity dissolves, and you reach the stage of total dissolution, mere vibration. Then your attention can move easily from the head to the feet and back again without any obstruction. This is what I refer to as "sweeping."

So sweeping occurs when you are totally clear.

Totally—when there is no blockage anywhere. The Buddha says: "By this technique, a student learns how to feel the entire body in one breath. Breathing in, you feel the entire body. Breathing out, you feel the entire body." This happens only when the body dissolves, when all solidity disappears. Then as you breathe out, you feel from head to feet; as you breathe in, you feel from feet to head. That is what we call sweeping—a stage where the body dissolves and intense mental contents dissolve as well. If there are strong emotions, you can't get this sweeping, because strong emotions result in a feeling of solidity in the body. When emotions are dissolved at the mental level, and the solidity of the body is dissolved at the material level, nothing remains but a mass of vibration, a mass of energy moving in the body.

Ideally, one would be able to do this all the time, throughout the day.

Yes. Once one reaches this stage, one continues to work with sweeping. But certain conditionings or impurities of the past, called sankharas, may exist at a very deep level of the mind. Through this sweeping, moving from head to feet and feet to head, these impurities get shaken and start coming to the surface. Say a certain sankhara manifests itself as gross sensations in the body. You work on these gross sensations by just observing them, until they too dissolve and you again get a free flow.

The goal of this technique is not to achieve the free flow of vibrations, which is after all just another transitory experience, but to accept with equanimity whatever manifests itself. In this way, you eradicate your mental conditioning layer by layer, and along with it your suffering.

How is this practice different from other forms of vipassana?

I don't want to give any opinions about others. But as I understand the teachings of the Buddha in the *Satipatthana Sutta* and elsewhere, the starting point can be different for different people, but at a certain stage everyone must follow the same path to nibbana. At the start of practice, Buddha gave different objects of meditation to different people, according to their mental conditioning, temperament, understanding, and capability. For example, those who have great attachment to the body and to the passions of the body, Buddha would have contemplate a corpse, so they would come to understand that their body is also like that — made up of flesh and bones and blood and pus and mucus and so forth. Someone who is so attached to the body doesn't want to accept that the body is dirty, after all. What, then, would there be to develop an attachment toward?

One can start this way, but eventually one must reach the stage where one experiences *anicca*, impermanence, how things arise and pass away. This arising and passing away should not be accepted at the intellectual or devotional level only; Buddha wanted us to experience it for ourselves. And it can be experienced only with sensation in the body. At the level of sensation, one finds, "Look, it has arisen, and look, it has passed away." Sensation arises, passes away; arises, passes away. When it is solidified, intensified, it arises and seems to stay for a while; but sooner or later it passes away. When all solidity dissolves, it turns into subtle vibration, and every vibration becomes a wavelet that arises and passes away.

So one experiences both solid sensation and subtle sensation arising and passing, arising and passing. Unless one experiences this directly, one hasn't understood the Buddha properly. Even before the Buddha, there were those who taught that the whole universe is impermanent, arising and passing. But Buddha discovered a technique by which one can experience it. And when we experience it, attachment, craving, and aversion go away, and the mind becomes purified. At a later stage, arising and passing occur so rapidly that one can't separate the one from the other. Then, after further purification of the mind, one reaches the stage of nibbana. Whether one starts with contemplating a corpse, the material parts of the body, respiration, or some other object, the rest of the path must be the same.

So this is why you stress mindfulness of sensation, as opposed to mindfulness of mental states.

Exactly. According to Buddha, whatever arises in the mind manifests itself as a sensation in the body. People don't give enough importance to this teaching. If you just observe mental states, that will help you to perfect your faculty of observation. But that is not the totality of the truth. You are observing only your thoughts. But what is happening to the body at that time? Mind and matter—both have to be observed.

When a thought arises, simultaneously there is a sensation in the body. And the sensation is actually the root of the problem. We don't react to thoughts. It may appear that, when I have a very pleasant thought in my mind, I start craving, and when I have a very unpleasant thought in my mind, I start to develop aversion. In fact, however, according to the law of nature, what you call a pleasant thought is nothing but a pleasant sensation in the body. Displeasure is nothing but an unpleasant sensation in the body. If you miss the sensation, you are just working at a surface level. This may give some benefit, but it won't take you where Buddha wanted you to go, to the stage where you eradicate your impurities. The roots still remain.

So when you are meditating, and you have a lot of mental turbulence . . .

Start observing the sensation in the body, and accept the fact that there is turbulence in the mind. That's all. Don't go into the details of the turbulence, and don't try to forcibly calm it down. Otherwise, you'll end up rolling around in your thoughts and not observing them objectively.

As you observe your sensation, you will find that your mind automatically calms down. Negativity is not suppressed, nor do you express it at the physical or vocal level. It just gets eradicated. If you observe the sensations with equanimity, without reacting to them, then you are purifying your mind at the deepest level. Otherwise you purify your mind at the surface level only.

Many of these ideas, which are classic Dhamma, foreshadow the insights of modern mind-body theorists. For example, the German psychologist Wilhelm Reich believed that past conditioning is stored in the body and can be released by working at the physical level. And Carl Jung, the Swiss psychologist, believed that the unconscious exists in the body.

Quite so. The so-called unconscious mind is constantly reacting to the body's sensations, while the conscious mind has no idea what is happening. There is a big barrier. The conscious mind may not know what the unconscious is doing. This technique breaks the barrier between the conscious and the unconscious. Then one becomes aware of everything that is happening in the body. Little sensations here or there that the conscious mind would not otherwise have felt, it now feels. And this technique trains the mind not to react. At the root level, the unconscious mind has always reacted with craving and aversion, and this influences the conscious mind as well. The entire structure of the mind is influenced by the root. Buddha teaches us that, if we rectify things at the root, the entire mind will become perfectly all right.

Unless the sleeping impurities at the root of the mind are eradicated, one can't call oneself an enlightened person. To me, Buddha's contribution to meditation was this technique by which the unconscious impurities are eradicated. Otherwise, the unconscious mind will always be reacting to the body sensation.

We've talked quite a bit about anicca, impermanence. What about the teaching of anatta, which is ordinarily understood as "no self" or "no abiding self"? Ordinarily we think that we need a self in order to function in the world. We have expressions like "self-esteem" and "self-confidence," and we believe that "ego strength" is a measure of a person's ability to cope with daily life. What does this "no self" teaching mean?

For those who haven't experienced the stage of "no self," it's true that in the apparent world there must be an ego, and this ego must be stimulated. If I don't crave something, I won't get the stimulation I need to function. In my courses, whenever I say that craving and attachment are harmful, people say that if there were no attachment, no craving, what would be the fun of living? There would be no life. We'd all be like vegetables.

Being a family man who has done business in the world, I can understand their concerns. But I also understand that when you work with this technique and reach the stage where the ego dissolves, the capacity to work increases manifold. When you lead a very ego-centered life, your whole attitude is to do as much as possible for yourself. But this attitude makes you so tense that you feel miserable. When, as a result of doing vipassana, the ego dissolves, then by nature the mind is full of love, compassion, and goodwill. You feel like working, not only for your own benefit, but for the benefit of all. When the narrow-minded ego stimulation goes away, you feel so much more relaxed, and so much more capable of working. This is my own experience, and the experience of so many who have walked on this path.

This technique does not make you inactive. A responsible person in society is full of action. What goes away is the habit of blind reaction. When you work with reaction, you generate misery. When you work without reaction, you generate positive feeling.

How do you recommend that people use this technique in their daily lives?

The first thing is to strengthen and perfect sila, morality. The five precepts we teach—no killing, no stealing, no sexual misconduct, no lying, no becoming intoxicated—are the base. Once one starts slipping in any of these, samadhi becomes weak, and panna becomes shallow. You can't work at the level of your sensations; you just end up playing intellectual games at the surface of the mind. But if sila is strong, you can start going to the depths of the mind. And then, when you've gone to the depths and eradicated even some of the impurities, sila and samadhi are both strengthened. All three help each other.

The next thing is this: While you're working, give all your attention to your work. That is your meditation at that time. But when you're free, even for five minutes, be aware of your sensations with open eyes. Whenever you have nothing else to do, observe your sensations. This will give you strength while you are going about your tasks. This is how people can use this technique in their daily life.

What about enlightenment. Where does enlightenment figure into all of this?

To me, enlightenment is progressive. It is because of ignorance that we keep on reacting deep inside with craving and aversion. When we come to understand that we are craving in reaction to a pleasant sensation and feeling aversion in reaction to an unpleasant sensation, then we have become enlightened to that reality. As we proceed, this reality becomes clearer and clearer, which means that enlightenment is increasing. And as we explore this path of arising and passing, arising and passing, we experience something that is beyond arising and passing, which we call nibbana.

So enlightenment is the experience of a state beyond arising and passing.

Yes, final, complete enlightenment is the experience beyond mind and matter, beyond the entire sensorium. All sense faculties stop working there. Eyes, ears, nose, tongue, body, mind— hey cannot function. For all practical purposes, one is like a dead person. But deep inside one is aware. How one is aware, and what one is aware of, cannot be explained in words, because the experience is beyond the sensory field.

So a person like this doesn't function in the world.

Yes, while one is in that state—for a second, or a few minutes, or maybe even a few hours—one does not function. Then one comes back to the sensory field, but one is totally changed. Because now one understands everything at the experiential level.

Having had that experience, a person would then lead a very different life.

Yes. That is an important yardstick for measuring whether one is enlightened or not. Otherwise anybody can say, "I reached this or that stage." But the only way to judge is to examine how they lead their life.

Jean Klein

Jean Klein is a master of *advaita vedanta*, the philosophical culmination of the Hindu tradition. According to this teaching of ultimate nondualism, the entire universe is, in essence, a single reality—consciousness, the true Self of all beings—to which each of us is inherently capable of awakening.

Like his illustrious predecessors in this century, Ramana Maharshi (1879-1950) and Sri Nisargadatta Maharaj (1897-1981), Klein does not draw on the terminology or doctrine of any tradition, but instead speaks directly from his own experience. Indeed, he is constantly seeking new ways to express the inexpressible, realizing that if he uses a word or a phrase too long, his students will attach to it and thus fail to see the reality to which it merely refers. In true advaita fashion (and much like the "direct pointing" of the early Zen masters), his utterances themselves have the capacity to open our eyes, if only for an instant, to our essential nature.

In person, Jean Klein has the vigor, freshness, and attentive curiosity of a child. He speaks English slowly, with an accent that blends his native Czech, the German of his school days, and the French he has spoken in France and Switzerland since before the war. Of his early background he talks little, believing it to be of no importance in the critical work of realizing our true nature.

In his latest book, *Transmission of the Flame,* he does admit to an idyllic early home life in Czechoslovakia (and later Vienna) between the wars, where he developed his lifelong fascination with music and began practicing the violin. At the University of Berlin, he continued his study of music while also preparing for the practice of medicine. When the Nazis came to power, he fled with his family to France and then Algeria, where they remained for the duration of the war.

But the inner search, which had begun inside him as an adolescent, found no fulfillment in the West, and in the early 1950s Klein packed up his wife and two daughters and moved to India, where he hoped to find a culture that encouraged self-inquiry. In Bangalore, not long after he arrived, he met a Sanskrit professor who impressed him with his gentle openness, humility, and lack of striving. After several visits, this teacher, whom he called Pandiji, introduced Klein to a direct perception of his real nature, which, over the course of three years, he was able to deepen and clarify.

During this period, Klein lived very intensely in not-knowing, looking at the world with openness and receptivity "without formulating conclusions." He also continued to have regular contact with Pandiji, which took the form of lengthy conversations that "exhausted thinking" as well as times of just being together in silence. "His being was the transmission," Klein says. "In a real teacher, this is all transmission is."

Then, one day in Bombay, Klein looked up at some flying birds and immediately found himself permanently awake in the openness which before had only been a transient state.

In 1957, at Pandiji's suggestions, Klein returned to Europe to share his realization with others. Yet over the years he has established no centers or organizations. Instead, he prefers to travel from place to place answering questions and teaching his special brand of hatha yoga to those who gather, in six European countries and the United States, to study with him. Six collections of his dialogues have been published, including *Who Am I?* and *The Ease of Being.*

The approach to yoga Klein teaches, which he calls body work, or the body approach, is a gentle, nondirective exploration of the interface between the physical body and the energy or subtle body. "Stay with the feeling," he advises students as he leads them in asanas or preparatory poses. "Don't get caught in effort or end-gaining. Keep the feeling alive."

The goal, according to Klein, is not greater flexibility or alignment, but rather a body and mind that are relaxed, open, spacious, and thereby more receptive to spiritual insight or awakening. Indeed, hatha yoga is little more than a "pedagogical device" for Klein, a skillful means in the larger work of "transmitting the flame" of self-realization. Yet he is dedicated to this "pastime," as he calls it, and his teaching style is at once energetic and precise.

Klein first became interested in the connection between thought, feeling, and movement while studying music and medicine at the university. Before leaving for India, he had already begun exploring "certain movements for channeling the dispersed energy in the body," and while studying with Pandiji he journeyed several times to learn hatha yoga from the world-renowned pundit Sri Krishnamacharya. He also received guidance in the Kashmir approach to working with the energy body from a wandering *muni* [silent sage] he met in Bangalore. But he is quick to point out that, although these two men helped him refine his understanding of the body, he had only one true teacher, the one who introduced him to the nature of reality.

Jean Klein

Be Who You Are

Jean, I find you and your teaching interesting for a number of reasons. For one thing, you are a Westerner who went to India long before such journeys were common and ended up attaining a high degree of realization. What prompted you to go to India?

I was hoping to find a society where people lived without conflict. Also, I think, I was hoping to find a center in myself that was free from conflict—a kind of forefeeling, or foretaste, of truth.

While in India, you found a teacher with whom you studied for a number of years. What is the value of a teacher for the spiritual life?

A teacher is one who lives free from the idea or image of being somebody. There's only function; there's no one who functions. It's a loving relationship; a teacher is like a friend.

Why is that important for someone on the spiritual path?

Because generally the relationship with other people involves asking or demanding—sex, money, psychological or biological security. Then suddenly you meet someone who doesn't ask or demand anything of you; there's only giving.

A true teacher doesn't take himself for a teacher, and he doesn't take his pupil for a pupil. When neither one takes himself to be something, there is a coming together, a oneness. And in this oneness, transmission takes place. Otherwise the teacher will remain a teacher through the pupil, and the pupil will always remain a pupil.

When the image of being something is absent, one is completely in the world but not of the world; completely in society, but at the same time free from society. We are truly a creative element when we can be in society in this way.

What did your teacher teach you?

The teacher brings clarity of mind. That's very important. There comes a moment when the mind has no reference and just stops, naturally, simply. There's a silence which you more and more live knowingly.

And the teacher shows you how to do that. Did you learn any meditation or yoga techniques from your teacher?

No. Because what you really are is never achieved through technique.

You go away from what you are when you use technique.

What about the whole notion of the spiritual path—the idea that you enter a path, follow a certain prescribed way of practice, and eventually achieve some goal?

It belongs to psychology, to the realm of the mind. These are sweets for the mind.

What about the argument that if you don't practice, you can't attain anything?

You must first see that in all practice you project a goal, a result. And in projecting a result you remain constantly in the representation of what you project. What you *are* fundamentally is a natural giving up. When the mind becomes clear, there is a giving up, a stillness, fulfilled with a current of love. As long as there's a meditator, there's no meditation. When the meditator disappears, there is meditation.

So by practicing some meditation technique, you are somehow interfering with that giving up.

Absolutely.

How?

You interfere because you think there is something to attain. But in reality what you *are* fundamentally is nothing to obtain, nothing to achieve. You can only achieve something that remains in the mind, knowledge. You must see the difference. Being yourself has nothing to do with accumulating knowledge.

In certain traditions—Zen, for one—you have to meditate in order to exhaust the mind; through meditating the mind eventually wears itself out and comes to rest. Then a kind of opening takes place. But you're suggesting that the process of meditating somehow gets in the way of this opening.

Yes. This practicing is still produced by will. For me, the point of meditation is only to look for the meditator. When we find out that the meditator, the one who looks for God, for beauty, for peace, is only a product of the brain and that there is therefore nothing to find, there is a giving up. What remains is a current of silence. You can never come to this silence through practice, through achievement. Enlightenment—being understanding—is instantaneous.

Once you've attained this enlightenment or this current, do you then exist in it all the time?

Constantly. But it's not a state. When there's a state, there is mind.

So in the midst of this current there is also activity?

Oh, yes. Activity and nonactivity. Timeless awareness is the life behind all activity and nonactivity. Activity and nonactivity are more or less superimpositions upon this constrain beingness. It is behind the three states of waking, dreaming, and sleeping, beyond inhalation and exhalation. Of course, the words "beyond" and "behind" have a spatial connotation that does not belong to this beingness.

In the midst of all activity, then, you are aware of this presence, this clarity.

Yes, "presence" is a good word. You *are* presence, but you are not aware of it.

You've often called what you teach the direct way, and you've contrasted it with what you call progressive teachings, including the classical yoga tradition and most forms of Buddhism. What is the danger of progressive teachings, and why do you think the direct way is closer to the truth?

In the progressive way, you use various techniques and gradually attain higher and higher states. But you remain constantly in the mind, in the subject-object relationship. Even when you give up the last object, you still remain in the duality of subject and object. You are still in a kind of blank state, and this blank state itself becomes an extremely subtle object. In this state, it is very difficult to give up the subject-object relationship. Once you've attained it, you're locked into it, fixed to it. There's a kind of quietness, but there's no flavor, no taste. To bring you to the point where the object vanishes and you abide in this beingness, a tremendous teacher or exceptional circumstances are necessary.

In the direct approach, you face the ultimate directly, and the conditioning gradually loses its impact. But that takes time.

So the ultimate melts the conditioning.

Yes. There's a giving up, and in the end you remain in beingness.

You say that any kind of practice is a hindrance, but at the same time you suggest practices to people. You teach a form of yoga to your students, and to some you recommend self-inquiry, such as the question, "Who am I?" It sounds paradoxical—no practice, but you teach a practice. What practices do you teach, and why do you use practices at all?

To try to practice and to try not to practice are both practice. I would rather say listen, be attentive, and see that you really are *not* attentive. When you see in certain moments in daily life that you are not attentive, in those moments you are attentive. Then see how you function. That is very important. Be completely objective. Don't judge, compare, criticize, evaluate. Become more and more accustomed to listening. Listen to your body, without judging, without reference—just listen. Listen to all the situations in daily life. Listen from the whole mind, not from a mind divided by positive and negative. Look from the whole, the global. Students generally observe that most of the time they are not in this listening, although our natural way of behavior is listening.

The path you are describing is often called the "high path with no railing," which is the most difficult path of all. The average person wouldn't know where to begin to do what you're talking about. Most could probably be attentive to their inattention, but after that, what? There's nothing to grasp onto.

No, there's nothing to grasp, nothing to find. But it is only apparently a difficult path; actually, I would say it is the easiest path.

How so?

Listening to something is easy, because it doesn't go through the mind. It is our natural behavior. Evaluation, comparison, is very difficult, because it involves mental effort. In this listening there's a welcoming of all that happens, an unfolding, and this unfolding, this welcoming, is timeless. All that you welcome appears in this timelessness, and there's a moment when you feel yourself timeless, feel yourself in welcoming, feel yourself in listening, in attention. Because attention has its own taste, its own flavor. There's attention to something, but there's also attention in which there's no object: nothing to see, nothing to hear, nothing to touch, only attention.

And in that moment of pure attention, you realize the one who's being attentive?

I would say that this attention, completely free from choice and reflection, refers to itself. Because it is essentially timeless.

The Zen master Dogen said: "Take the backward step that turns your light inwardly to illuminate the self." That seems to be similar to what you are talking about.

Yes, but one must be careful. Turning the head inward is still doing something. And there's really no inward and no outward.

I notice that you use the word "attention." Is this the same as what the Buddhists call mindfulness—being acutely aware of every movement, every sensation, every thought?

Mindfulness mainly empathizes the object, the perceived, and not the perceiving, which can never be an object, just as the eye can never see its seeing. The attention I'm speaking of is objectless, directionless, and in it all that is perceived exists potentially. Mindfulness implies a subject-object relation, but attention is nondual. Mindfulness is intentional; attention is the real state of the mind, free from volition.

What about the yoga you teach, which you call "body work?" What is it, and why do you teach it?

You are not your body, senses, and mind; body, senses, and mind are expressions of your timeless awareness. But to completely understand that you are not something, you must first see what you are not. You cannot say "I am not the body" without knowing what it is. So you inquire, you explore, you look, you listen. And you discover that you know only certain fractions of your body, certain sensations, and these are more or less reactions, resistance. Eventually you come to a body feeling that you have never had before, because when you listen it unfolds, and the sensitive body, the energy body, appears. It is most important to feel and come into contact with the energy body. Because in the beginning your body is more or less a pattern or superficial structure in the mind, made up of reactions and resistance. But when you really listen to the body, you are no longer an accomplice to these reactions, and the body comes to its natural feeling, which is emptiness. The real body in its original state is emptiness, a completely vacant state. Then you feel the appearance of the elastic body, which is the energy body. When we speak of "body work," it is mainly to find this energy body. Once the energy body has been experienced, the physical body works completely differently. The muscle structure, the skin, the flesh, is seen and felt in a completely new way. Even the muscles and bones function differently.

What is the yoga that you teach like?

It's not really yoga. It's an approach to the body based on the Kashmir teaching. The Kashmir approach is largely an awakening of the subtle energies circulating in the body. These energies are used to spiritualize the body, to make it more *sattvic* [literally, "pure" or "true"]. In a sattvic body there is already a giving up. You see more clearly what you are not—your tensions, ideas, fixations, reactions. Once the false is seen as false, what remains is our timeless being. By spiritualizing the body, therefore, I mean orchestrating all the dispersed energy that belongs to the false. Our approach is an exploration without will or effort. It is inspired by the truth itself. The natural body is an expression, a prolongation, of this truth.

But I understand you use the traditional asanas of hatha yoga.

Every gesture, every position the body can take, is an asana; there are certain archetypes that are not even mentioned in the classical texts of hatha yoga. But there are archetypal positions par excellence that bring the harmonization of body and mind. Before going to these archetypes, however, one must prepare the body. There is no point in assuming these archetypes in a conditioned body. Otherwise, yoga is nothing more than a kind of gesticulation. What you see for the most part in Europe and the U.S. is gymnastics, gesticulation, and has nothing to do with body integration.

Do you have any other reasons for not using the term "yoga"?

Yes. The term "yoga" means to "to join," and so there must be something to join, something to attain. But join who? Join what? In a certain way the body approach helps you to listen quietly. It is through real listening to the body that you come to true equanimity of mind and body.

Should this be practiced every day?

Don't make a discipline of it, because in discipline there is anticipation—you're already emphasizing a goal. This doesn't belong to exploration.

Practically speaking, wait until you are invited by the energy of the body itself. This recall of our natural state is not memory. It comes from the needs of the body and appears spontaneously. Go to it as you would to a dinner invitation. Otherwise, you're doing violence to the body.

In your daily life you may experience moments of absolute silence in which there's nothing to do, nothing to avoid, nothing to achieve. In these moments, you're completely attuned to this stillness without any effort. Become more and more aware of these timeless moments, moments when you cannot think, because when you think, the moment is already past. Present moments free from all thoughts. Often you will have these moments when an action is accomplished, when a thought is finished, in the evening before you fall asleep, in the morning when you first wake up. Become more and more familiar with these gaps between two thoughts or two actions—gaps which are not an absence of thought, but are presence itself. Simply let yourself be attuned to these timeless moments. You will increasingly welcome them, until one day you are established in this timelessness, are knowingly the light behind all perceptions.

So you don't recommend practicing meditation as a regular discipline?

No.

You talk about stillness and silence. Are these goals of spiritual life?

When I speak of stillness and silence, nobody is still and nobody is silent; there is only silence and stillness. This stillness does not refer to somebody or something.

So in the midst of this stillness there is activity?

Yes. Stillness is like the hinge of a door. The body is the door that opens and closes constantly, but the stillness never moves.

T. S. Eliot called it "the still point of the turning world." Since the practice has no goal—in fact, there isn't even a practice—what is the purpose of spiritual life at all? Obviously, most of us would say that we are not enlightened or liberated, and so we do feel a need to go somewhere where we are not. Then it seems as if we do need to undertake some kind of spiritual life. What is that like?

I would say that we are constantly, without knowing it, being solicited by what we *are* fundamentally. But the feeling by which we are solicited is very often mistaken for something objective, for a state, for some relative mental stillness that we can achieve through effort or practice. We seek this state as a kind of compensation for real stillness. The moment you are really solicited by the inner need and you face it and visit with it, you will be taken to it. But generally we are looking for compensation.

This process you're talking about is very different from the way we usually do things. Usually we have an idea in mind of where we are going and then we set out in a certain direction and use our will to get there.

But all doing has a certain motive. I think this motive is to be free—free from oneself, free from all conflict.

The motive is a good one, then, but the response is a little misguided.

When you become more and more acquainted with the art of

observation, you will first see that you do not observe; when you see that you don't observe, you are immediately out of the process. There is a moment, a kind of insight, when you see yourself free from all volition, free from all representation; you feel yourself in this fullness, in this moment beyond thought. It's mainly through observation and attention that you come to feel what you *are* fundamentally.

How would you describe liberation?

I'll give you a short answer. It is being free from yourself, free from the image you believe yourself to be. That is liberation. It's quite an explosion to see that you are nothing, and then to live completely attuned to this nothingness. The body approach I teach is more or less a beautiful pretext, because in a certain way the body is like a musical instrument that you have to tune.

And we tune it to play on it the song of our own nothingness.

Exactly. Liberation means to live freely in the beauty of your absence. You see at one moment that there is nothing seen and no seer. Then you live it.

This is what you refer to as living free from psychological memory.

Absolutely.

Is it really possible to live in the world in this state of total openness and freedom from our own identity, doing the things we do—leading busy lives, taking care of family, etc.?

Yes. You can live in a family perfectly without the image of being a father or a mother, a lover or a husband. You can perfectly educate your children not to be something, and have a love relationship with them as friend, rather that as a parent.

One teacher of vipassana meditation who is also a clinical psychologist has written, "You have to be somebody before you can be nobody," meaning that for many people, particularly now in the West, who have been brought up in dysfunctional families, there are very often such deep psychological problems, such a deep lack of self-esteem and such a conflicted or uncertain sense of who they are in an everyday way, that they must first develop psychological and emotional strength before they can embark on the path to becoming nobody. There are people who would hear you say that ultimately we have no identity, we are nothing, and we live in this nothingness, and would turn around and say, "Oh, yes, I know that." What they are really talking about is their own inner emptiness, their own inner feeling of lack or deprivation, which is a kind or sickness. Do you agree that we have to be somebody before we can be nobody?

First you must see how you function. And you will see that you function as somebody, as a person. You live constantly in choice. You live completely in the psychological structure of like and dislike, which brings you sorrow. You must see that. If you identify yourself with your personality, it means you identify yourself as your memory because personality is memory, what I call psychological memory. In this seeing, this natural giving up, the personality goes away. And when you live in this nothingness, something completely different emerges. Instead of seeing life in terms of the projections of your personality, things appear in your life as they are, as facts. And these appearings naturally bring their own solution. You are no longer identified with your personality, with psychological memory, though your functional memory remains. Instead, there is a cosmic personality, a trans-personality, that appears and disappears when you need it. You are nothing more than a channel, responding according to the situation.